# stitch graffiti

## X X UNEXPECTED CROSS-STITCH X X

Heather Holland-Daly

INTERWEAVE PRESS.
interweavebooks.com

Photography by Joe Coca

Text © 2008 Heather Holland-Daly
Technical Editing by Deanna Hall West
Photography © 2008 Interweave Press LLC
Illustrations © 2008 Interweave Press LLC

Interweave Press LLC
201 East Fourth Street
Loveland, CO 80537-5655 USA
interweavebooks.com

Printed in China by Asia Pacific Offset

Library of Congress Cataloging-in-Publication Data

Holland-Daly, Heather, 1966-
  Stitch graffiti : unexpected cross-stitch / Heather Holland-Daly,
author.
    p. cm.
  Includes index.
  ISBN-13: 978-1-59668-045-6 (pbk.)
  1. Cross-stitch--Patterns.  I. Title.
  TT778.C76H654 2008
  746.44'3041--dc22
                                    2007027319

10  9  8  7  6  5  4  3  2  1

# acknowledgments

This book is dedicated to my husband, Tim, and our three-year-old son, Myles, who gave me space to create plus helped me finish many projects in this book; Mom, who gave me the world of stitching, art, and music; Grandma Madeline for giving me the stitching lesson; and Dad (who seems to believe I finally have a "real" job) for reading me poetry when I was a kid instead of watching TV; my sister Sarah (aka Scary), who stitched for me into the wee hours, and her family Charlie, Truman, and Winifred for giving her the time to stitch; and Alicey, who I miss every day.

I want to thank Tricia Waddell, Ann Budd, and all the talent at Interweave Press who gave me the spark and support to do this book.

Thanks also goes out to Don Urban, my lawyer and friend; My Model Stitchers Sharon Schutjer, Jessica Gagnon, and Kim Mattox, who, along with my sister Scary, executed my designs with perfection; and the Gustafson family for helping to entertain my child and listen to my long to-do lists.

A special thanks also to Karen Galer and all of the gals (and Larry) at Mom & Me for constant support and encouragement. You will be missed.

# contents

## The whys, what fors, and whens of the matter at hand

Once upon a time, counted-thread embroidery was a part of everyday life. Needlework was taught alongside grammar and arithmetic to prepare young girls for a successful life of caring for their family's clothing and other household needs (such as bedding and table linens). Before that, it was passed down for generations from mother to daughter, as it often is now. I came to love the craft because my mother and grandmother did such beautiful stitching. My grandma was one of those schoolgirls who found a lifelong love for needle arts at school and passed her love and knowledge on to me. Although some people might look at these designs and say, "This is not your Granny's cross-stitch," I wholeheartedly disagree. It is. It's the same basic stitch—a simple "×" made by crossing two stitches and grouping these crossed stitches on countable evenweave fabric to create words or images. I like to make the × by first taking a stitch from the lower left to the upper right (/), then crossing the first leg with another stitch from the lower right to the upper left (\), but you can do them in the opposite order just as well (just be consistent in how you make the stitches).

What has changed are the supplies. Today, we stitch largely for leisure, not necessity. We stitch for relaxation, to make personal gifts for friends and relatives, to decorate our clothing and homes, or to simply keep our hands and mind out of trouble! Whatever the reason, the sense of creation and accomplishment is as rewarding now as it was then.

# The Supplies

### aka, The Stash

Although the stitches remain the same, the stuff of cross-stitch has changed. The flower children of the 1960s and their parents—like my mother and grandma—who helped resurrect the popularity of cross-stitch would be thrilled. The fabric is still evenweave and the thread is still mostly 6-strand cotton floss, but the selection is vast now. There are specialty needlework shops both online and throughout the country. There are fabrics in many different counts and threads of different fibers—silk, cotton, wool, just to name a few. And the colors! You can get every color under the rainbow in solid, variegated, and beautifully handdyed options.

### The Designs

Cross-stitch designs are still printed on gridded charts, but they have moved beyond the teddy bears and country look of the 1980s and the traditional samplers of alphabets and verses that have been passed down through the centuries. Although those patterns still have a place, it's time to add new ideas. My goal is to bring a new generation of stitchers to the craft and to inspire stitchers of old to pick up a needle and stitch again! I intend to whet your stitching appetite and excite you to share it with a friend, who in turn will share it with another friend, and so on. . . . Pay it forward, if you will. Hey, "pay it forward" would make a pretty cool cross-stitch design.

### The Fabric

There are lots of fabrics (and non-fabrics) that work for cross-stitch. The most common are single-weave cotton and linen, but don't overlook other fabrics such as Aida, Hetherfield, Betsy Ross linen, and Klostern.

*Evenweave* Evenweave is a woven fabric that has the same number of vertical threads as horizontal threads per inch of fabric. The fabric forms a woven grid with small holes between adjacent threads. To cross-stitch you simply bring a threaded needle in and out of the fabric through these holes, following a charted design for color placement. Most designs specify that you stitch over one or two threads of fabric. If you stitch over one thread, you'll stitch from hole to hole over one thread of the fabric for each cross-stitch. Stitching over one thread is most often done on linen and other plain-weave fabrics. If you stitch over two threads, you will enclose a 2-by-2 group of fabric threads and there will be an empty hole in the center of each

There are lots of types of evenweave fabrics.

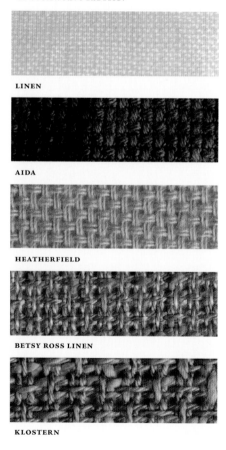

**LINEN**

**AIDA**

**HEATHERFIELD**

**BETSY ROSS LINEN**

**KLOSTERN**

completed cross-stitch. Stitching over two threads is most often done on plain-weave fabrics such as linen and Jobelan. But, you can choose to stitch over one or two threads whenever you want! The final design size can be reduced by half when stitching the design over one thread, if it originally called for stitching over two. This brings us to fabric thread counts, no wait, more fabric stuff!

*Waste canvas* Waste canvas comes in handy when you want to stitch a design onto any fabric that isn't evenweave (like blue jeans) or fabric that is exceptionally fine (like a lightweight cotton blouse). Baste the waste canvas on top of the fabric you want to stitch on, stitch your design over the waste canvas, then remove the threads of the waste canvas, and voilà—you have an evenweave design on non-evenweave fabric. Waste canvas comes in counts like 10, 12, and 14 stitches per inch. It's easiest to pull out the waste-canvas threads once the piece has been dampened or washed to dilute the fabric sizing, so it's best to stitch the design with a washable thread, such as DMC cotton floss.

*Screen* Yep, that's right. Screen—the synthetic or wire kind you get from a hardware store or you find lying around the basement or workshop just waiting to be chosen for a needle-art project! The number of "threads" or "strands" per inch in screens is not an exact science in the hardware industry, but most seem to be close to 18 count and may not be an evenweave. Screen is actually quite easy to stitch on—I've taught kids to do it. But I'd recommend only two types of threads for stitching on screen: Caron Collection Watercolours, which is a handdyed, 3-stranded thread (use just 1 strand) and size 5 pearl cotton (I prefer Weeks Dye Works, but DMC works well, too). These three brands offer a vast variety of colors that should cover all your screen-stitching bases! Cool stuff.

Waste canvas and screen are good alternatives to standard cross-stitch fabrics.

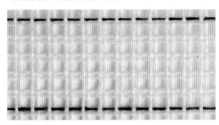

**12-COUNT WASTE CANVAS**

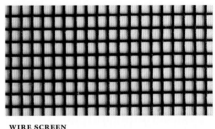

**10-COUNT WASTE CANVAS**

**WIRE SCREEN**

*move forward . . . always move forward!*

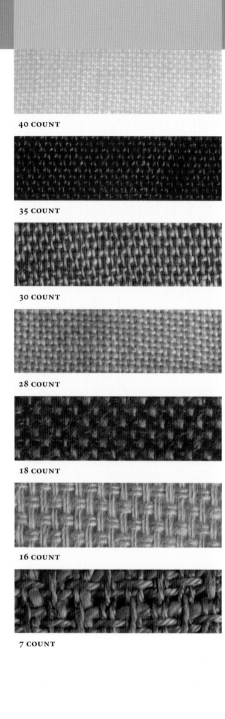

**40 COUNT**

**35 COUNT**

**30 COUNT**

**28 COUNT**

**18 COUNT**

**16 COUNT**

**7 COUNT**

***Counts*** The fabric count is a measure of how many threads there are in one inch of fabric. To measure the count, just place a ruler on top of the fabric and count the number of threads widthwise or lengthwise in an inch. The fabric count lets you determine the final dimensions of a stitched design, which is particularly helpful if you plan to buy a frame for your completed stitchery. Knowing the stitch count also helps you decide which size needle to use, how many strands of thread to use, and how much thread you'll need. Fabrics counts come in 8, 10, 14, 16, 18, 20, 24, 28, 30, 32, 35, 36, and 40 counts (and probably a few in between that I missed). A 10-count fabric has large, easy-to-see holes between the threads; 40-count fabric has itsy-bitsy, teeny-weeny holes between the threads. A design stitched on 10 count over 1 thread (i.e., each × is made across a single thread of the fabric) will be much larger than the same design stitched on 18-count fabric over 1 thread. Also, if you stitch on 28 count over 2 threads (i.e., each × is made across 2 threads of the fabric), the finished design will be the same size as if you stitched on 14 count over 1 thread.

If you want to figure out the size of a design on a particular fabric, you just need to do a little elementary math (it's not hard, I promise). Let's say your design is 78 stitches wide by 156 stitches tall and you want to use 28-count fabric.

We know that for 28-count fabric, there are 28 threads per inch. If you want to stitch the design over 1 thread, the width of the design will be 78 stitches ÷ 28 stitches/inch = 2.8". The length will be 156 stitches ÷ 28 stitches/inch = 5.6". So, your design will end up 2.8" wide by 5.6" high. For simplicity, round these numbers up to whole inches: 3" wide by 6" high.

If you want to stitch the same design over 2 threads, the width will be 78 stitches ÷ 14 stitches/inch = 5.6". The length will be 156 stitches ÷ 14 stitches/inch = 11.2". Again, for simplicity, round these numbers up to 6" wide by 12" long.

*just a little elementary math . . .*

When purchasing fabric, you'll want to add about 3" to all sides of the design so you'll have plenty of extra fabric surrounding the design for framing or sewing onto a pillow. For an example, if you plan to stitch our previous example design over 1 thread, you'll need a piece of fabric that's 3" + 6" = 9" wide by 6" + 6" = 12" long; if you plan to work over 2 threads, you'll need a piece of fabric that's 6" + 6" = 12" wide by 12" + 6" = 18" high.

I promise that this is the most difficult part of cross-stitch. Don't worry; you will get the hang of it. For safety, I always round up when deciding the size of the fabric—you know how it goes: bigger is better; better safe than sorry; a bird in hand is worth two in the bush; yadda, yadda, yadda.

THE IMAGE ON THE LEFT WAS STITCHED OVER ONE THREAD; THE IMAGE ON THE RIGHT WAS STITCHED OVER TWO.

## The Threads

Okay, I have to be completely honest here. I am, have long been, and will likely always be, a thread junkie. My attraction to the feel, textures, and vast array of colors is only rivaled by my newfound, similarly addictive attraction to beads. I could probably write an entire book on why I love thread, but then I wouldn't have any time to play with it, look at it, and revel in it. My thread collection is vast because of the easy availability of most threads. I have lost my perspective, though not my understanding, of the limits of one's pocketbook. However, I've tried to limit the projects in this book to threads that are widely available and reasonably priced. One of my favorites is 6-strand cotton floss by DMC. It comes in a huge variety of solid colors as well as variegated ones. It is reasonably priced, easy to find, and washable.

But don't overlook the beautiful handdyed, handpainted, and overdyed threads that are also available. Although they are not all colorfast (and do not claim to be; check the label) and may require dry cleaning, they provide a depth of color that just can't be duplicated with other threads. For many of the projects in this book that specify handdyed threads, I provide alternative colors in DMC floss. If you do substitute, be aware that the design may look significantly different. On the other hand, you could substitute hand-dyed thread for the projects that specify solidly colored DMC floss and give a whole new look to those designs.

Embroidery threads are typically manufactured in combinations of strands—anywhere from a single strand to 12 (or more). Depending on the thickness of the individual strands and the count of the cloth you're working on, you may want to use a single strand of thread or several strands to give the appropriate coverage. For example, 14-count cloth has large holes that will require several strands of a fine thread or a single strand of a thick thread. The project instructions will specify the thread density (i.e., 1 strand of thread over 2 strands of cloth, 2 strands of thread over 1 strand of cloth, etc.). When you're ready to stitch, just cut a length of thread, then separate out the appropriate number of strands to work with.

## The Needles

Of course, you'll need a needle. Tapestry needles are blunt tipped, large-eyed needles that come in a variety of sizes, which like wire, are scaled so that usually the smaller numbers refer to larger sizes. For example, a size 26 needle is smaller than a size 20. In addition, you can get them in "petite" sizes that are slightly shorter than the regular ones. I particularly like petite needles for stitching on linen. Tapestry needles come in stainless steel, platinum, or gold-plated. Play around with different types to see what you like best: I prefer stainless steel; my sister swears by gold. The needles I specify for the projects in this book are the needles that worked best for me—ultimately, you should decide the size that you like best. In general, use a size 22 or 24 needle when working on screen. Use a size 26 needle when working on Aida cloth, Heatherfield, 24-count banding, and 20- and 24-count linen. Use a size 28 needle when working on 28- to 40-count linen. Use a sharp needle when working on waste canvas.

Be glad that the days of pin and needle shortages are long gone. During the revolutionary war, women made saltpeter for gunpowder that was in turn bartered for precious needles and pins. Without these necessary stitchery accessories, Betsy Ross might never have been able to stitch her famous flag! You have lots of choices. Enjoy them and experiment!

## The Hoops

Not! You don't need one. That's right—no hoop! If your design is larger than your hoop, you run the risk of the hoop leaving telltale smashed stitches. Besides, you may find that it's a whole lot easier to get the correct tension for your thread if you can insert the needle into the fabric and out again in the same motion (rather than down and out in two steps, as you would if the fabric were stretched in a hoop). Just be careful not to pull the stitches too tightly or you'll get unsightly holes in the ground fabric at the corners of the cross-stitches, and be careful not to let the stitching threads twist too much or you'll get uneven fabric coverage.

[LARGER THAN ACTUAL SIZE]

SIZE 28 NEEDLES IN
GOLD AND STAINLESS STEEL

SIZE 26 NEEDLES IN
REGULAR AND PETITE

SIZE 24 NEEDLE IN
STAINLESS STEEL

## Scissors

You'll want a sharp pair of embroidery scissors with narrow points that can fit under individual stitches. To keep your scissors sharp, never use them to cut anything but fabric and thread—using them to cut paper will quickly make them dull. I attached a beaded fob onto my embroidery scissors so everyone knows that they are mine and off limits. For traveling on airplanes, I use a Clover Cutter, which is a safe razor-blade cutter that looks like a pendant. This cutter won't work for fabric, so be sure to cut the fabric prior to your trip.

# Your Creativity

Now, here's the thing; you could follow all of the instructions in this book word for word and make your projects look exactly like the ones in the photos or you can take some liberties. Remember that the finished piece is yours or yours to give, not mine. The designs might be mine, but there's no reason you can't substitute a different color or type of thread or fabric. Don't get tied down to my decisions—feel free to change any aspect of any design. The point of stitching (or any craft) is for it to be fun and relaxing. Do what works for you!

If you do decide to make changes, keep in mind that the thread colors need to contrast with the fabric color for the stitches to show and that thread size or number of thread strands used must be appropriate for the fabric count. Before I begin a design, I usually lay all of the threads on top of the fabric to make sure they "pop" sufficiently. If one color doesn't quite work, I change it. I may make several changes before I'm happy with the overall effect. Only after I'm sure I like the combination of fabric and thread do I cut the fabric. This part of designing can be fun and addictive. You may find that you never use the threads or fabric specified!

*use your own creativity to make it sing!*

# Stitching with Handdyed Thread

Handdyed and variegated threads can take a little getting used to because the colors can group together in "pools" among the stitches. Different projects may call for different techniques. Try each to see which technique you prefer for your particular project.

**Stitch each cross-stitch around the perimeter, then fill in the center:** Complete each stitch individually around the outer perimeter of a block of color, forming a border, then stitch toward the center in a circular pattern. This approach was used for the top circle in the swatch at right. Notice how the color play creates a design within the circle design.

**Complete each cross-stitch as you stitch across a row:** Work both legs of each stitch (i.e., complete each stitch individually) before moving to the next stitch. This is the approach used for the center circle in the swatch. It has a tendency to produce a striped look, which you may or may not want.

**To get a tweed effect:** There are two ways to achieve the tweedy effect shown in the bottom circle. Both provide interesting looks and both are similar to blending together two shades of solid-color threads.

If you're stitching with two strands, you can align the strands so that the opposite ends of the thread lengths are placed together, creating a variegation of color which intentionally does not match, creating a tweedy appearance. For example, let's say you're using a thread that changes from red to purple to green, and you're using two strands that start with red and end with purple. Separate these two strands and turn one around so that the purple end aligns with the red end. The colors along the strands will not match up exactly. Use the thread in this orientation to finish each cross-stitch as you proceed.

Another way to achieve this look is to have the colors along the strands match so that red aligns with red, purple with purple, etc. Instead of completing each cross-stitch individually (as in the center circle), stitch just the first leg of each stitch across an entire row, then return by stitching only the remaining leg to complete each stitch.

STITCH AROUND THE PERIMETER, THEN FILL IN TO THE CENTER IN A SPIRAL PATTERN.

COMPLETE EACH STITCH INDIVIDUALLY IN A ROW.

STITCH ONE LEG OF EACH STITCH IN A ROW, THEN RETURN AND STITCH THE REMAINING LEGS.

## The Basic Stitch

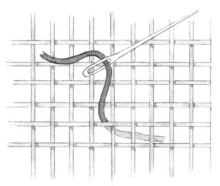

**FIGURE 1**

To begin, thread the desired number of strands into a tapestry needle. Insert the threaded needle into the fabric from back to front, then pull it through until a short tail of thread hangs from the back (Figure 1). Insert the needle in and out of the fabric to form a small thread loop on the back; catch the thread tail under the loop; and gently pull the thread to secure the tail (Figure 2). Secure the thread tail under several stitches.

Each cross-stitch is worked in two parts—the first leg leans from lower left to upper right (Figure 3), then the second leg is worked directly on top of the first, but this time it leans from lower right to upper left (Figure 4). You can complete each stitch individually before moving to the next stitch (Figure 5), or you can work a row of the first legs of the stitches followed by completing the stitches with the second legs (Figure 6).

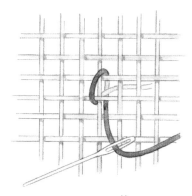

**FIGURE 2**

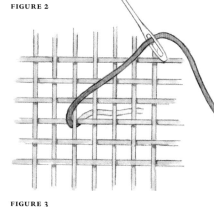

**FIGURE 3**

*hand-dyed linens and threads make for a home-spun look . . .*

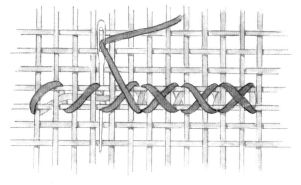

**FIGURE 4**

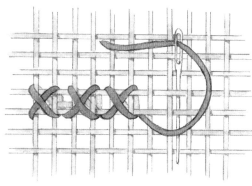

**FIGURE 5**

**FIGURE 6**

To form cross-stitches "over 1 thread," work each stitch over a single thread of the background fabric (Figure 7). To form cross-stitches "over 2 threads," work each stitch over 2 threads of the background fabric (Figure 8). In general, when stitching with overdyed and variegated threads, it's a good idea to complete both legs of a stitch before going on to the next one. However, you can get some interesting effects by not following this standard (see Stitching With Handdyed Thread on page 15).

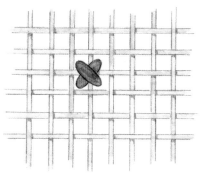

FIGURE 7

When you get to the end of a length of thread, turn the fabric over, and run the needle through the backs of about 5 stitches (Figure 9) to secure it. Trim the tail close to the stitches.

Place another length of thread into your needle and continue where you left off by starting your new length of thread by burying the tail into the backs of previously worked stitches. If you're using handdyed thread, you'll want to be sure that the new length of thread begins at the same place in the color sequence where the old thread ended. For example, if the handdyed thread changes from red to purple to green then back to red, and you ended with a green stitch, you'll want to have the first stitch of the new strand be the same shade of green as the ending stitch. This means that you may have to trim off the red and purple to get to the right spot in the color sequence. This will keep the color gradations consistent and the stitches will look as though they were all worked with a single length of thread.

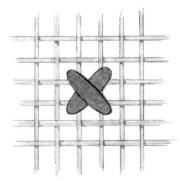

FIGURE 8

## Finishing

There's no end to how you can finish your needlework—sew it onto a pillow or bag, frame it, adorn some clothing. Take a trip to your local craft store for ideas. You'll find readymade frames, pillows, and bags, or the supplies to make your own. Look for beads, buttons, paint, rubber stamps—anything that can be used for embellishment. You can also find many treasures at the hardware store, auctions, or swap meets. Consider game pieces like dominoes, mah-jongg or Scrabble tiles, or Monopoly charms. Armed with a glue gun, you'll be ready to attach anything that can't be stitched in place.

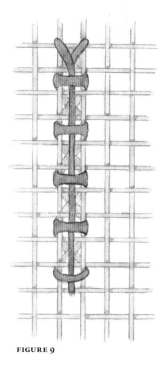

FIGURE 9

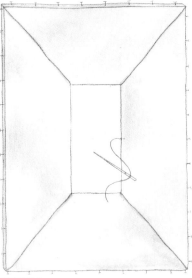

**FIGURE 1**

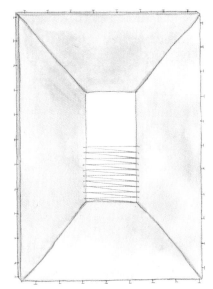

**FIGURE 2**

## Pressing

No matter how you intend to finish your piece, it will need to be pressed. Place your needlework right side down on a clean terry-cloth towel. Set your iron to the appropriate setting, and when it is fully heated, iron the wrong side of the needlework. This will prevent you from smashing or catching the stitches on the front. If you stitched on handdyed fabric or used hand-dyed threads, do not use the steam setting. Steam might cause the colors to change or run. I know—I've done it. Simply iron the piece with no steam, pressing firmly and moving the iron constantly. You could also lightly mist the fabric around the stitching and press it smoother. If your fabric and threads are colorfast, go ahead and use the steam setting (or handwash the stitchery in tepid water with a mild laundry soap and rinse several times before pressing to remove all traces of dirt and hand oils).

## Framing

I often choose to paint my frames, whether I buy them readymade at the craft or hardware store or make them myself. I've found the latex paints with an eggshell finish work best. I seem to have a harder time getting glossy paint to look as nice.

*Lacing* If you want to mount or frame your needlework, you'll want to stretch and lace it over a piece of mat board. Mat board is available at craft and art supply shops and is easily cut with a mat knife. For framing, you'll want to cut the mat board to fit snugly (allowing for the thickness of the fabric) inside the frame. Glue a single layer of polyester fleece to the top of the mat board to cushion the stitches so that they sit level with the mat board, not above it. Place and center your pressed needlework on top of the cut, fleece-covered mat board. Hold the stitchery in place on the board with T-pins, aligning one fabric thread per side along the edge of the board. Carefully turn the piece over and place it right side down on a clean surface. Thread a tapestry needle (the color doesn't matter—it won't show in the end) and anchor the thread at the center of one side of the fabric, using the same method you did to start threads for stitching (Figure 1). Following a path similar to lacing shoes, stitch the opposite sides of the fabric together, working from the center to one edge with a fairly tight and even tension (Figure 2), then secure the thread. Begin again at the center and work to the opposite edge (Figure 3). Turn the piece over to check that the design is still centered on the mat board and correct the placement, if necessary. Lace the remaining two fabric sides together in the same way (Figure 4), checking often to make sure that the design remains centered. When finished lacing, remove the T-pins. The fabric should be taut without wrinkles or sags, and the design should be centered over the mat board.

***Sandwich Frames*** A nice alternative to a conventional frame is a sandwich frame (see Bloomer, page 90). It's easy to make and can have all the personality of your needlework. You'll need two thin pieces of wood (about the thickness of a wooden ruler and about 2" wider than the finished fabric); a hand drill with drill bit; two nuts; two bolts to match the size of the drill bit (the exact size doesn't really matter; they just have to be compatible); two washers; and stain or paint. First, drill a hole about one-half inch in from the end of each piece of wood. Stain or paint the wood as desired (or recycle a piece of barn wood or molding that doesn't need staining). When the paint or stain is dry, center the pressed stitched fabric between the two pieces of wood and centered between the holes, place the bolts through the predrilled holes, thread the nuts on the bolts, and tighten the nuts.

This makes a versatile frame. You can easily change what's in it. You can stitch four seasonal pieces and change them out quarterly; or you can alternate hanging different designs so you never get tired of them. Another cool feature is that you get creative with what you use for washers. I used gears in the Bloomer design on page 90, but you can use anything that you can drill a hole through—buttons, bottle caps, coins, poker chips, pieces of broken pottery—the sky's the limit!

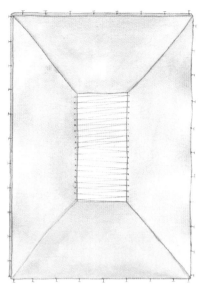

FIGURE 3

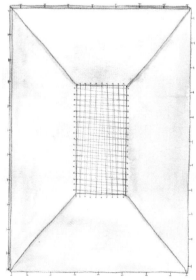

FIGURE 4

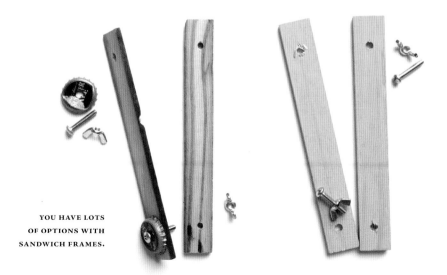

**YOU HAVE LOTS OF OPTIONS WITH SANDWICH FRAMES.**

# Stitching My Way

Whenever I stitch, I associate certain truths to my designs and possibilities for variations. I also inevitably associate some song or tune with the time I spent stitching, and by the time I'm finished with a design, I think of different ways that the words can be interpreted. I've included these tidbits with each project, both to help you see how it evolved and to give you fuel for your own creative variations.

### Truths [troothz]

noun, plural. **1.** the true or actual state of a matter **2.** honesty; integrity; truthfulness **3.** a verified or indisputable fact, proposition, principle, or the like **4.** the state or character of being true

*These Truths are mine and mine alone. They explain how I got an idea in the first place, or why it took shape and was stitched, or what became interesting about the design as it evolved into the image you see in this book. Even if you choose to stitch one of these designs exactly as I have, you'll find your own truths that attracted you to it or came to be while you worked it. Those truths are yours and yours alone and will make your stitching your own.*

### Tunes [tyoonz]

noun, plural **1.** a melody, especially a simple and easily remembered one **2.** a song **3.** archaic frame of mind; disposition

> Yes, The Rhythm Of Life is a powerful beat,
> To feel The Rhythm Of Life,
> To feel the powerful beat,
> To feel the tingle in your fingers,
> To feel the tingle in your feet.
> —"The Rhythm of Life" from Sweet Charity
> by Cy Coleman, Dorothy Fields, and Neil Simon

*Something settles in my brain every time I stitch a piece and that association will come rushing back whenever I look at the finished project. It's like remembering what was playing on the radio when you got your first kiss or like smelling some-*

*thing in the air that takes you right back to summer camp. The tunes I list with the projects are simply ones that gave me the idea for the designs or ones that were playing on my iPod while I was stitching. Create your own stitch tunes or step outside your box and tune your ear to something new, as well as your fingertips!*

## Possibilities [pos-uh-bil-i-teez]

*noun, plural.* **1.** the fact or state of being possible **2.** something that is possible **3.** potentiality for favorable or interesting results: The idea has great possibilities

*When I refer to possibilities, I hope to spark your own thoughts and ideas. My possibilities will give you suggestions and ideas on how to use, stitch, or finish the design, whether it's to modify the design provided or to be transferred onto a completely different project. I hope to give you possibilities that spark ideas for your very own creations.*

## Definitions [def-uh-nish-uhnz]

*noun, plural.* **1.** the act of defining or making definite, distinct, or clear **2.** the formal statement of the meaning or significance of a word, phrase, etc. **3.** the condition of being definite, distinct, or clearly outlined

*I'm fascinated with how language is interpreted. I include definitions to the names of the patterns simply as food for thought—the same word can generate completely different connotation to different people. It's quite possible that a word or phrase will have a different meaning to you than it does to me. I find this fascinating. These definitions provide yet another layer of possibilities.*

# Here We Go

So now you are all set to start stitching. If you weren't an "old pro" before, you are now—equipped with all the information you need to make this a successful journey! There are many other things to learn and discover along the way, so hang on and enjoy the ride.

Whenever I stitch, I associate certain truths to my designs and possibilities for variations.

## Graffiti [gruh-fee-tee] ~ noun

1. markings, as initials, slogans, or drawings, written, spray-painted, or sketched on a sidewalk, wall of a building or public restroom, or the like  2. an ancient drawing or writing scratched on a wall or other surface  3. A drawing or inscription made on a wall or other surface, usually so as to be seen by the public

# graffiti

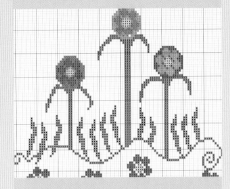

## Graffiti with thread instead of spray paint.

Mark up your home or office with quotes, initials, and observations that are meaningful to you. Enjoy stitching these using the alphabet on page 108 to put your own words into stitches.

# W'hirled Peas

## Possibilities

Do you believe it's possible that we hear words like "evil," "terror," "war," etc. . . . more than we hear the word "peace"? The human mind is a powerful tool—imagine if everyone in the world truly believed in world peace. Visualize it. Imagine what that would be like. Peace . . .

## Truths

A rebound college boyfriend had a dream of starting his own T-shirt biz. He had dozens of drawings for the graphics and wording that he eagerly showed me late one rainy night. I don't know what became of him, but when I saw a "imagine whirled peas" T-shirt on a teenager in a mall, I had to wonder.

## Finishing

Press and insert into frame as described on page 18. The frame shown here is just a lonely old frame I found at an auction. I painted it lavender, then rubbed off some of the paint before it had completely dried. Just like white-wash, except with purple paint!

STITCHING TUNES
Ella Fitzgerald, "Rogers and Hart songbook." Ella is simply amazing— upbeat and mellow at the same time.

*peace* [pees] *noun*

*1. a state of mutual harmony between people or groups  2. untroubled; tranquil; content  3. inner contentment*

## IMPORTANT STUFF

### Fabric
R&R Reproduction 30-count Handdyed Apricot Linen: 14" (35.5 cm) wide by 15" (38 cm) high.

### Thread
Crescent Colours Handdyed 6-strand Cotton Floss: Pansy Purple, Blooming Crocus, Cashmere, Blue Beadboard, Blueberry Tart, Granny Annie, Rainy Day, Boysenberry Jam.

### Stitch Density
2 strands of thread over 2 fabric threads.

### Stitch Count
107 wide by 126 high.

### Design Size
7¾" (19.5 cm) wide by 8½" (21.5 cm) high.

### Extras
Frame with 7½" x 9½" (19.5 x 24 cm) opening.

| Crescent Colours | DMC alternate | | Crescent Colours | DMC alternate | |
|---|---|---|---|---|---|
| CASHMERE | 211 | LIGHT LAVENDER | PANSY PURPLE | 550 | VERY DARK VIOLET |
| BLUE BEADBOARD | 794 | LIGHT CORNFLOWER BLUE | BOYSENBERRY JAM | 3607 | LIGHT PLUM |
| BLOOMING CROCUS | 208 | VERY DARK LAVENDER | RAINY DAY | 315 | DARK PLUM |
| BLUEBERRY TART | 3840 | LIGHT LAVENDER BLUE | GRANNY ANNIE | 798 | DARK DELFT BLUE |

# Kiss

## Possibilities

Some additional fun finishing ideas would be to stitch this design using waste canvas onto an apron or to find an old frame (or make or buy one), paint it black, and glue utensils all over it. You could also find old wooden spoons, cut off the handles, and nail or glue them to a frame. There are many possibilities for creativity with this design.

*Salsa*
3 big fat tomatoes, diced
1 bunch of the freshest cilantro you can find
    (sometimes this is tricky)
1 medium-ish red onion, finely diced
5 cloves of crushed garlic (or a heaping teaspoon of
    crushed garlic from a jar)
2 squirts of lime juice
1–3 dashes of balsamic vinegar
sprinkle of sugar, to taste
sprinkle of salt

Mix all ingredients. Add a fresh peach (if in season) or a ripe avocado just before serving, if desired.
Serve with blue corn chips.

This is how we cook at my house . . . it explains a lot.

*kiss [kis] verb*

*1. to join lips in respect, affection, love, passion, etc.: They kissed passionately  2. to express a thought, feeling, etc., by a contact of the lips, "she loved her finished project so much she just had to kiss it!"  3. to purse and then part the lips, emitting a smacking sound. Something a two-year-old masters early on*

## IMPORTANT STUFF

### Fabric
Wichelt Imports 16-count Natural Heatherfield: 14" (35.5 cm) wide by 14" (35.5 cm) high.

### Thread
Crescent Colours Handdyed 6-strand Cotton Floss: Fancy Nancy Green, Really Teally, Grape Pie, Ripe Melon, Little Pink Peony.

### Stitch Density
3 strands of thread over 2 fabric threads.

### Stitch Count
117 wide by 107 high.

### Design Size
7½" (19 cm) wide by 7" (18 cm) high.

### Extras
Chalkboard frame (made by monsterbubbles for this design).

## Truths

The idea for this design came from a little hotel bar/restaurant that was attached to the Travel Lodge on Historic Route 66 in Flagstaff, Arizona. The food was fine, the service was average, but the atmosphere was amazing. It could be that I was taking a big personal journey as well as a long drive from Nashville, Tennessee, to Bakersfield, California, with my three cats in my little Honda, or it really might have been the atmosphere. A sign next to the entrance to the kitchen read "I kiss better than I cook." I did not stay long enough to find out, but I wouldn't be surprised.

## Finishing

Press and insert into frame portion of chalkboard frame as described on page 18.

STITCHING TUNES
Ben Harper and the Innocent Criminals, "I Always Have to Steal My Kisses From You." It always makes me think of that trip.

## Crescent Colours | DMC alternate

 GRAPE PIE — 552 MEDIUM VIOLET

**5** REALLY TEALLY — 3845 MEDIUM BRIGHT TURQUOISE

▭ FANCY NANCY GREEN — 991 DARK AQUAMARINE

✶ LITTLE PINK PEONY — 761 LIGHT SALMON

**2** RIPE MELON — 3832 MEDIUM RASPBERRY

# Jolly

## Possibilities

What does it take to make you holly jolly, or just jolly? Make a list! What is holly jolly, anyhow? As Jack Skelington said in "A Nightmare Before Christmas" when trying to use the scientific method to figure out what Christmas was, "But what does it mean?!"

## Truths

Christmas time always brings a barrage of memories. When I hear the Christmas tune "Holly Jolly Christmas," it brings me back to a time when I was in the second or third grade and how excited I was to watch holiday specials on TV. It was a big event in our house—we just didn't watch TV all that much. This was the mid 1970s, too, before cable and videos, which made these shows even more special. I always looked forward to broadcasts of *The Grinch Who Stole Christmas*, but my favorite Christmas show by far was *Rudolph, the Red Nosed Reindeer*. I cherish memories of hearing Burl Ives belt out " . . . I don't know if there'll be snow, but have a cup of cheer."

## Pillow Finishing

Cut the design linen 1" (2.5 cm) from the stitching on all sides, being careful to follow a single line of holes along each side. Pin the linen to the center of the mustard wool, making sure it doesn't pucker. Cut the wool fabric 2" (5 cm) larger than the linen on all sides. Set the mustard wool aside. Carefully pull out 12 threads on all sides of the linen to create a fringe. Pin the linen piece to the full fat quarter of red wool, centering it and making sure

*jolly* [jol-ee] *adjective*

*1. cheerfully festive  2. joyous; happy*

*3. in good spirits; merry*

**IMPORTANT STUFF**

### Fabric
R&R Reproduction 30-count Hand-dyed Parchment Linen: 14" (35.5 cm) wide by 17" (43 cm) high for pillow; 10" (25.5 cm) wide by 11" (28 cm) high for hanging.

### Thread
The Gentle Art Sampler Threads 6-strand Cotton Floss: Forest Glade, Spring Grass, Black Crow, Buckeye Scarlet, Parchment, Slate, Midnight, Gold Leaf.

### Stitch Density
**Pillow:** 2 strands of thread over 2 fabric threads. **Hanging:** 1 strand of thread over 1 fabric thread.

### Stitch Count
127 wide by 161 high.

### Design Size
**Pillow:** 8" (20.5 cm) wide by 11" (28 cm) high. **Hanging:** 4" (10 cm) wide by 5" (12.5 cm) high.

### Extras
**Pillow:** Weeks Dye Work wool fabric: #1224a Mustard and #2268a HT Candy Apple, 1 fat quarter each (about 20" [51 cm] square); one 5M spool Kreinik #4 braid in #8 Green; Thread Heaven thread conditioner or beeswax (available at fabric stores); pillow stuffing.
**Wall Hanging:** Foam-core board 1" (2.5 cm) larger than finished design on all sides; polyester fleece; multicolored push-pins.

it is flat and evenly lined up with the herringbone stripes. Use one strand of the Kreinik #4 braid to attach the linen to the wool (you may want to treat the braid with thread conditioner or beeswax to make the stitching easier and to help reduce tangles). Keeping all starting threads on the back side of the wool, stitch large uneven cross-stitches about every inch or so around the linen, paying no attention to uniformity—willy nilly is the idea! Center the mustard wool on the wrong side of the red wool and pin it in place. Connect the two pieces by sewing cross-stitches (willy nilly as before), remembering to keep all the loose thread tails on the side that will become the inside of the pillow and leaving an opening for stuffing the pillow. To do this, after you have stitched a cross-stitch on both the front and back, go in through the mustard wool and run the thread between the two pieces of wool to the position of the next stitch so that the long stitches are hidden between the cross-stitches. Loosely stuff the pillow with fiberfill, then close the opening with more cross-stitches. Knot the thread to one of the long stitches on the inside and trim the thread as short as possible. Stitch the thread tail into the inside of the pillow. Remove pins. Trim the edges of the red wool in a free-form curvy pattern, making sure that the mustard wool is not visible from the front.

You now have a fun pillow to help keep the holiday mood festive or a jolly gift to lighten the demeanor of any grinch!

## Wall Hanging Finishing

Cut the foam-core board 1" (2.5 cm) larger than the finished design size on all sides. Fold and lace the fabric edges to the back, keeping the design centered (see page 18). Stick the push-pins as close as possible into the board's edge around all sides. This is a fun and inexpensive way to display a stitched piece. Give it to your new favorite person this year!

STITCHING TUNES
Harry Connick, JR.,
"When My Heart
Finds Christmas,"
and "The Amy Grant
Christmas Album."

| | Sampler Threads | DMC alternate | |
|---|---|---|---|
| ✖ | MIDNIGHT | 3842 | DARK WEDGEWOOD |
| m | GOLD LEAF | 3854 | MEDIUM AUTUMN GOLD |
| | BUCKEYE SCARLET | 326 | VERY DARK ROSE |
| 8 | SLATE | 415 | PEARL GRAY |
| | BLACK CROW | 311 | MEDIUM NAVY BLUE |
| | FOREST GLADE | 986 | VERY DARK FOREST GREEN |
| ≡ | SPRING GRASS | 989 | FOREST GREEN |
| ♥ | PARCHMENT | 312 | VERY DARK BABY BLUE |

# Truth

## Truths

"Truth" comes from something I saw written on a chalkboard in a booth at a craft fair in southern Illinois. The booth had all kinds of cute "bling-blings" and inspiration. Right next to the cash drawer the artist had jotted down "follow your truth" for no apparent reason. I must have been going through something meaningful at the time because the phrase stuck with me. Anyway, it's a good way to live.

## Finishing

Fold fabric edges to back, allowing ½" (1.3 cm) margins from stitched design. Press. Handstitch design to pillow using sewing thread to match design fabric. Attach buttons.

*truth* [trooth]  *noun*
*1. the true or actual state of a matter, "she told the truth about how much cross-stitch stash she bought" 2. a verified or indisputable fact, proposition, principle*

**IMPORTANT STUFF**

**Fabric**
Mill Hill 24-count Pumpkin and Tangerine Woven Checks Stitch Band: 8¼" (21 cm) wide by 16" (40.5 cm) high.

**Thread**
The Gentle Art Sampler Threads 6-strand Cotton Floss: Royal Purple, Spring Grass, Buckeye Scarlet, Hyacinth, Deep Sea, Hibiscus.

**Stitch Density**
2 strands of thread over 1 fabric thread.

**Stitch Count**
106 wide by 268 high.

**Design Size**
4½" (11.5 cm) wide by 11¼" (28.5 cm) high.

**Extras**
10" x 16" (25.5 x 40.5 cm) pillow (pillow shown is Pumpkin Love from Trail Creek Farm; it comes with matching buttons).

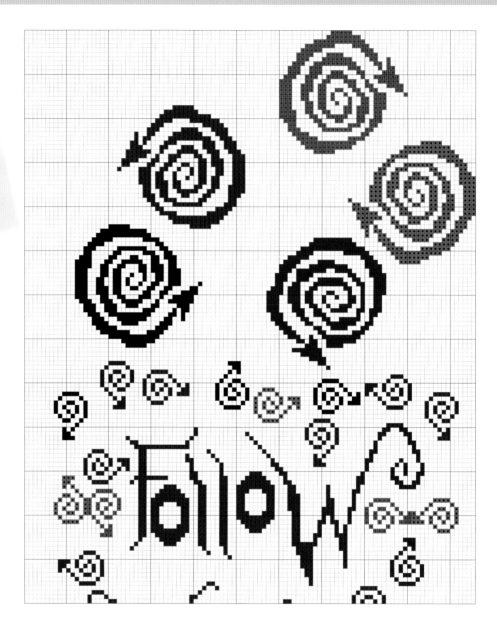

| Sampler Threads | DMC alternate | |
|---|---|---|
| HIBISCUS | 3806 | LIGHT CYCLAMEN PINK |
| DEEP SEA | 796 | DARK ROYAL BLUE |
| SPRING GRASS | 906 | MEDIUM PARROT GREEN |
| HYACINTH | 3834 | DARK GRAPE |
| BUCKEYE SCARLET | 321 | RED |
| ROYAL PURPLE | 939 | VERY DARK NAVY |

# flowers

## Possibilities

Wouldn't this design be cute hanging above your garden tools? Or make your own frame with hooks to hang your tools. Maybe stitch it up for your best gardener buddy? Stitch a single flower or stitch all three on different pieces of fabric, frame them in identical frames, and hang them in a row. Change the colors! So much to stitch, so little time—hey, that might make a cute cross-stitch, too!

## Truths

Ralph Waldo Emerson was an American poet who was born in Boston in 1803 and died in 1882. He was buried in Sleepy Hollow Cemetery in Concord, Massachusetts. He was known not only for his poetry and writings but also known for his founding of the Transcendental Club, which served as a center for the transcendental movement. This quote is one of his most famous and copied.

## Finishing

Press design and mount as described on page 18.

*laugh [laff] verb*

*1. to express mirth, pleasure, derision, or nervousness with an audible, vocal expulsion of air from the lungs that can range from a loud burst of sound to a series of quiet chuckles and is usually accompanied by characteristic facial and bodily movements 2. to experience the emotion so expressed: She laughed inwardly when she saw what a big mistake she made!*

### IMPORTANT STUFF

**Fabric**
R&R Reproduction 30-count Handdyed Dawn's Early Light Linen: 14" (35.5 cm) wide by 15" (38 cm) high.

**Thread**
Crescent Colours Handdyed 6-strand Cotton Floss: Cobbles Peach, Ceruse, Tangerine, Eve's Leaves, Frozen Margarita, Tomatillo, Cloud.

**Stitch Density**
2 strands of thread over 2 fabric threads.

**Stitch Count**
157 wide by 113 high.

**Design Size**
9¼" (23.5 cm) wide by 6½" (16.5 cm) high.

**Extras**
Frame with 9" x 9" (23 x 23 cm) opening (frame shown is from Hog River); polyester fleece fabric.

**Crescent Colours**    **DMC alternate**

| | | | |
|---|---|---|---|
| ▣ | COBBLES PEACH | 818 | BABY PINK |
| ◥ | CERUSE | 605 | VERY LIGHT CRANBERRY |
| ⊞ | TANGERINE | 3825 | PALE PUMPKIN |
| 2 | EVE'S LEAVES | 895 | VERY HUNTER GREEN |
| ● | TOMATILLO | 471 | VERY LIGHT AVOCADO GREEN |
| ＊ | FROZEN MARGARITA | 726 | LIGHT TOPAZ |
| r | CLOUD | 815 | MEDIUM GARNET |

STITCHING TUNES
Antonio Lucio
Vivaldi, "The
Four seasons," of
course!

# lipstick

## Possibilities

This design lends itself perfectly to be stitched on a Walker mesh bag—reserve it for your special lipsticks and makeup! Stitch it on one of those cool mesh Walker bags but do it over one thread so the design isn't as big as your head! Unless, of course, you're a makeup junkie as I was in my pre-child days—then you'll need a bag the size of your head.

## Truths

For several years in a row I did a show with a woman named Connie Champagne. I'm not sure why I didn't recognize this as a stage name right off the bat. Somehow, it just seemed like the right name for her. One show we did was called "Judy's Scary Little Christmas," which was based on the Judy Garland Christmas specials that were commonplace in the 1950s (complete with guests like Bing Crosby, Liberace, and Ethel Merman). Our show was set in the year 2000 and the celebrities find out at the end that they are all dead, and they remember how they died, as well as celebrate the opportunity to do a show again with the ol' gang. For the show, Ms. Champagne did a spot-on Garland imitation. She was so good, she won all of the LA critics' awards that year. This is one of her quotes—she had many, as well as many stories to tell.

*lipstick [lip-stik] noun*

*1. a crayon-like oil-based cosmetic used in coloring the lips, usually in a tubular container 2. an Americanism used to describe a small stick of waxy lip coloring enclosed in a cylindrical case*

### IMPORTANT STUFF

#### Fabric
Wichelt Imports 28-count Handdyed Raspberry Lite Jobelan: 12" (30.5 cm) wide by 16" (40.5 cm) high.

#### Thread
The Gentle Art Sampler Threads Handdyed 6-strand Cotton Floss: Poppy, Deep Sea, Spring Grass, Raspberry Parfait.

#### Stitch Density
2 strands of thread over 2 fabric threads.

#### Stitch Count
81 wide by 134 high.

#### Design Size
5¾" (14.5 cm) wide by 9½" (24 cm) high.

#### Extras
Frame with 6¾" x 11" (17 x 28 cm) opening with mat board; 6¾" x 11" (17 x 28 cm) polyester fleece; 2 packages of Cherry and 1 package each of Pink Lemonade and Black Cherry Kool-aid; 1 tube of pink-hued scrapbook beads (beads shown are Art Accentz in Chunky Glitter Party Pink from Provo Craft); craft glue suitable for wood and glass.

## Finishing

The frame is a monsterbubbles creation made out of molding we got from the local hardware store. Instead of painting it, I dyed it with Kool-aid! You can dye all kinds of fibers in Kool-aid as well as produce some bright happy colors. But beware that if your finished piece should find itself in direct sunlight, your Kool-aid-dyed frame could fade. For this frame, I literally opened up the pantry and grabbed the flavors I had on hand. The general recipe is one package Kool-aid mixed with 1½ cups of water. For a more intense color, use just ¼ cup of water. I mixed two packages of Cherry and one package each of Pink Lemonade and Black Cherry with 2 cups of water in a 9" × 11" (23 × 28 cm) baking pan. I placed the frame (front side down) in the pan, placed a weight on it (I used a water glass) to prevent it from floating, and let it soak for 2 hours, though I don't think the time is all that important. Rinse the frame lightly with tap water and let dry thoroughly. To attach the beads, draw a line of craft glue along the groove of the frame or ¼" (6 mm) in from the frame edge if no groove is present. Sprinkle the beads on top of the wet glue and gently pat the beads into the glue to help them adhere to the frame. Let dry overnight. Finish as described on page 18.

| Crescent Colours | DMC alternate | |
|---|---|---|
| ☐ POPPY | 760 | SALMON |
| ▦ RASPBERRY PARFAIT | 600 | VERY DARK CRANBERRY |
| ⊡ SPRING GRASS | 906 | MEDIUM PARROT GREEN |
| ■ DEEP SEA | 3765 | VERY DARK PEACOCK BLUE |

ALSO USE DEEP SEA TO BACKSTITCH BETWEEN VERTICAL COLUMNS OF CROSS-STITCHES IN THE WORD LIPSTICK.

# Harvest Moon

## Possibilities

Some other options for this design could be to frame it or to stitch it over 1 on 28-count fabric for a much smaller design.

## Truths

The song "Shine on Harvest Moon" reminds me of my grandmother, Madeline, a ninety-three-year-old woman who has a beautiful voice and memory for old song lyrics. She remembers lyrics and melodies that no one else has even heard of! At the first glance of the full orange moon that is so familiar in the waning months of summer, she will sing "shine on, shine on harvest moon." Even when grandma is no longer with us, I will hear her singing it in my mind.

## Finishing

Press. Use 1 strand of 970 Light Pumpkin thread to stitch a bead to the second leg of the cross-stitches where indicated on chart. Cut the stitched linen fabric 1¼" (3.2 cm) from the stitching on all sides, then pull out the linen threads one by one to create a ¾" (2 cm) fringe on all sides. Using 1 strand of 720 Dark Spice Orange thread, attach the design fabric to the pillow with straight stitches worked over 2 threads horizontally and vertically at each corner and the midpoints between.

*harvest moon [hahr-vist moon] noun*
*1. the moon at and about the period of fullness that is*
*nearest to the autumnal equinox*

### IMPORTANT STUFF

**Fabric**
Wichelt Imports 30-count Handdyed Antique Copper Jobelan: 12" (30.5 cm) wide by 13" (33 cm) high.

**Thread**
DMC 6-strand Cotton Floss: 312 Very Dark Baby Blue, 720 Dark Orange Spice, 738 Very Light Tan, 801 Dark Coffee Brown, 826 Medium Blue, 827 Very Light Blue, 970 Light Pumpkin, 996 Medium Electric Blue.

**Stitch Density**
2 strands of thread over 2 fabric threads.

**Stitch Count**
70 wide by 73 high.

**Design Size**
4¾" (12 cm) wide by 4¼" (11 cm) high.

**Extras**
47 size 11 lime glass seed beads; 12" x 12" (30.5 x 30.5 cm) pillow (pillow shown is from Trail Creek Farm; size 28 tapestry needle.

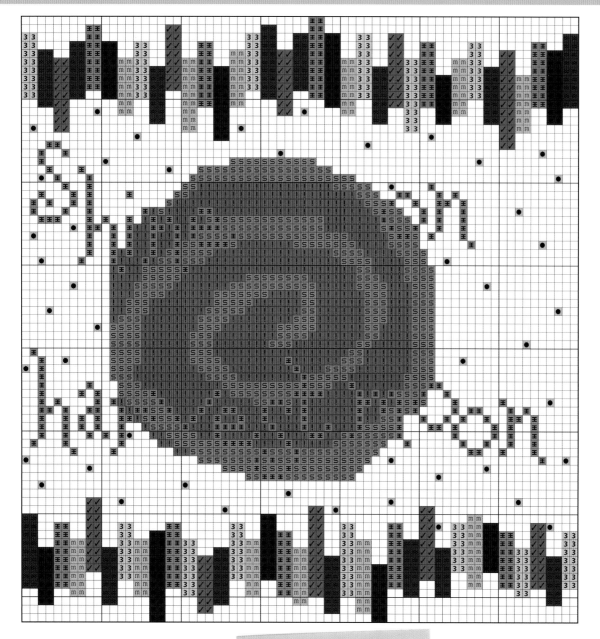

## DMC

| Symbol | Code | Name |
|---|---|---|
| S | 970 | LIGHT PUMPKIN |
| m | 827 | VERY LIGHT BLUE |
| !! | 720 | DARK ORANGE SPICE |
| ■ | 312 | VERY DARK BABY BLUE |
| ✓ | 826 | MEDIUM BLUE |
| ■ | 801 | DARK COFFEE BROWN |
| ⊞ | 996 | MEDIUM ELECTRIC BLUE |
| 3 | 738 | VERY LIGHT TAN |
| ● | | LIME SEED BEAD ON PUMPKIN THREAD |

STITCHING TUNES
Leon Redbone, "Double Time," which includes a great rendition of, what else?! "Shine on Harvest Moon."

# Relish

## Truths

I saw this quote in a funky shop in Laguna Beach, which was my favorite beach when I lived in California. The shop had all kinds of interesting jewelry, painted furniture, artwork, and the like. This phrase was stamped into a silver bracelet that caught my eye. The quote reminded me of the late nights I spent in college with my friends. Those nights seemed endless. Looking back, I don't have a clue how I functioned on so little sleep—especially now that I have a three-year-old! Funny how life is, isn't it?

## Finishing

To make your own starry frame, purchase an appropriately-sized wooden frame at a craft store and paint it dark gray. When the paint is dry, use a rubber stamp to stamp stars randomly placed with black ink. Pour embossing powder on the frame, let it sit for a minute, then pour it off (it helps to use a small brush to get the powder that tends to stick to the paint). Use an embossing gun about 6" (15 cm) above the frame to even out the paint color, using a circular motion so that the heat isn't pointed at one spot so long that it causes the paint to bubble. Mount design in frame as described in Finishing on page 18.

*relish* [rel-ish] *noun*

*1. hearty enjoyment; zest 2. a trace or suggestion of a pleasurable quality 3. a condiment of chopped sweet pickle*

STITCHING TUNES
The 5 satins, "In the Still of the Night," from the movie soundtrack to "Dirty Dancing."

### IMPORTANT STUFF

**Fabric**

R&R Reproduction 30-count Handdyed Pepper Linen: 15" (38 cm) wide by 16" (40.5 cm) high.

**Thread**

Crescent Colours Handdyed 6-strand Cotton Floss: Razzleberry, Finley Gold, Amber Waves, Sunshine Girl, Golden Star.

The Gentle Art Sampler Threads: Grecian Gold, Pineapple Sherbet, Harvest Basket, Gold Leaf.

**Stitch Density**

2 strands of thread over 2 fabric threads.

**Stitch Count**

131 wide by 152 high.

**Design Size**

8¾" (22 cm) wide by 10¼" (26 cm) high.

**Extras**

Frame with 9¼" x 11½" (23.5 x 29 cm) opening (frame shown was made by monsterbubbles for this design); polyester fleece.

relish the night...

| Crescent Colours | DMC alternate | | Sampler Threads | DMC alternate |
|---|---|---|---|---|
| **2** GOLDEN STAR | 307 | LEMON | **W** HARVEST BASKET | 3821 STRAW |
| **↘** SUNSHINE GIRL | 727 | LIGHT TOPAZ | **r** PINEAPPLE SHERBET | 3823 ULTRA PALE YELLOW |
| **S** AMBER WAVES | 728 | TOPAZ | **I** GRECIAN GOLD | 3822 LIGHT STRAW |
| **■** RAZZLEBERRY | 815 | GARNET MED | **÷** GOLD LEAF | 3046 YELLOW BEIGE |
| **♥** FINLEY GOLD | 745 | PALE YELLOW | | |

# Tattoos [ta-tooz] ~ noun

1. *a permanent mark or design made on the skin by a process of pricking and ingraining an indelible pigment or by raising scars* 2. *a permanent mark or design made on the skin by a process of pricking and ingraining an indelible pigment or by raising scars* 3. *a signal sounded on a drum or bugle to summon soldiers or sailors to their quarters at night*

# tattoos

## Live vicariously through your thread.

This is your chance to try that tattoo that you always wanted, but instead of your skin, print it on your jeans, jacket, purse, or wherever strikes your fancy. If you are all inked up, you know that choosing a tattoo is a personal process that requires careful thought and consideration. Try stitching a design on cloth first to see how you like it before you mark yourself permanently—take this opportunity to give a new tat a whirl and see how it wears!

# Biker Babe

## Truths

I think this would make a good tattoo. How many tattoos do you have? How many do you secretly want? Live vicariously through your stitching— tattoo your clothes instead.

## Finishing

Trim the stitched linen fabric about ¾" (2 cm) from all sides of the design (or more if you want longer fringe). Pull out the linen threads one by one all the way around to create a ½" (1.3 cm) fringe. Attach it to your jeans with two strands of Raven thread, working long straight stitches around the piece twice to secure the patch and prevent further fraying.

*biker babe [bi-ker beyb] noun*

*1. chicks on wheels 2. a movement of women that*
*ride motorcycles to show their equality to men*

## IMPORTANT STUFF

### Fabric
R&R Reproduction 30-count Handdyed Apricot Linen: 7" (18 cm) wide by 7" (18 cm) high.

### Thread
The Gentle Art Sampler Thread Handdyed 6-strand Cotton Floss: 7042 Raven and 7001 Barn Grey.

Kreinik #4 Very Fine Braid: #001 Silver.

### Stitch Density
3 strands of thread or 1 strand of braid over 1 fabric thread.

### Stitch Fabric
51 wide by 49 high.

### Design Size
2¼" wide by 2¼" high.

### Extras
A pair of old blue jeans.

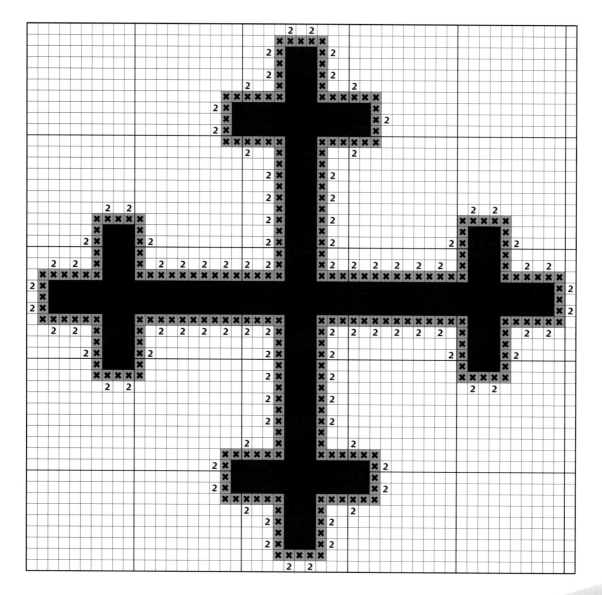

**Sampler Threads**
7042 RAVEN
7001 BARN GREY

**DMC alternate**
3371 BLACK BROWN
648 LIGHT BEAVER GREY

**Kreinik #4 Braid**
2   001 SILVER

**DMC alternate**
822 LIGHT BEIGE GREY

STITCHING TUNES
Sheryl Crowe,
"Tuesday Night
Music Club."

# Flower Child

This is great way to update an old top, a purse, or a pair of jeans.

## Truth

I have long been attracted to many aspects of the 1960s and love talking to people who were flower children. Stories of what is was like to be on the beaches in California or the parks in New York and San Francisco, are now sometimes hard to believe. Moreover, I love the fashion—the do-it-yourself styles. This flower is a tribute to those times—so decorate away!

## Finishing

Pin and baste waste canvas to garment and stitch design. After stitching is complete, wash the garment with the waste canvas still attached, then pull out the waste canvas threads one by one (as described on page 9) while the garment is still damp.

*flower child [flou-er chahyld] noun*

*1. a hippie, rejecting conventional society and advocating love, peace, and simple, idealistic values*

*2. a child of the 1960s*

**IMPORTANT STUFF**

**Fabric**

Waste Canvas, 12 count (available at craft and needlework stores): 14" (35.5 cm) wide by 15" (38 cm) high.

**Thread**

DMC Handdyed 6-strand Cotton Floss: 420 Dark Hazelnut Brown, 598 Light Turquoise (2 skeins), 744 Pale Yellow, 746 Off White (3 skeins), 988 Medium Forest Green, 3821 Straw.

**Stitch Density**

5 strands of thread over a 2-by-2 group of canvas threads.

**Stitch Count**

74 wide by 75 high.

**Design Size**

7¾" (19.5 cm) wide by 8½" (21.5 cm) high.

**Extras**

A plain blouse; straight pins to secure waste canvas to blouse.

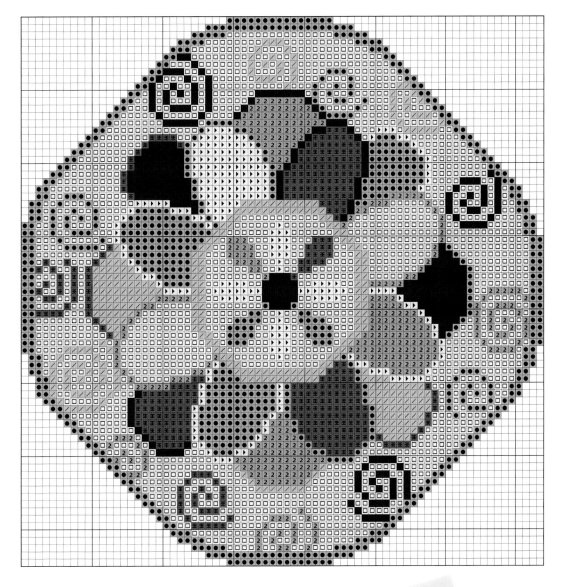

**DMC**

- ● 598 LIGHT TURQUOISE
- □ 746 OFF WHITE
- ⊞ 420 DARK HAZELNUT BROWN
- ╱ 3821 STRAW
- 2 988 MEDIUM FOREST GREEN
- ▶ 744 PALE YELLOW

STITCHING TUNES
Pete Seeger and
Arlo Guthrie,
"Together in
Concert."

# Cross My Heart

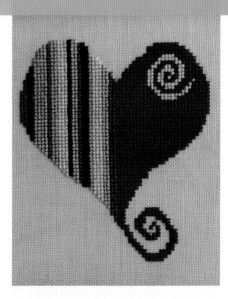

## Possibilities

What a nice Valentine's Day present this would make! You could add words such as "be mine," "you're mine," "that's mine, leave it alone," or something like that. This would be a great piece to experiment with different-count fabrics. If you stitched it over 1 on a light pink 20-count fabric, it would be the same size, but the look could totally change. Experiment!

## Finishing

Press and mount into frame as described on page 18.

*heart [bahrt] noun*

*1. a hollow, pumplike organ of blood circulation, composed mainly of muscle  2. the center of the total personality  3. spirit, courage, or enthusiasm  4. a red figure or shape on a playing card*

### IMPORTANT STUFF

**Fabric**
R&R Reproduction 40-count Handdyed Goldfinch Linen: 9" (23 cm) wide by 9" (23 cm) high.

**Thread**
DMC Handdyed 6-strand Cotton Floss: 208 Very Dark Lavender, 210 Medium Lavender, 814 Dark Garnet, 3708 Light Melon, 3747 Very Light Blue Violet, 3804 Cyclamen Pink.

**Stitch Density**
2 strands of thread over 2 fabric threads.

**Stitch Count**
55 wide by 62 high.

**Design Size**
2¾" (7 cm) wide by 3¼" (8.5 cm) high.

**Extras**
Frame with 4" x 6" (10 x 15 cm) opening.

**DMC**

| | |
|---|---|
| 208 | VERY DARK LAVENDER |
| 814 | DARK GARNET |
| 8 | 3708 LIGHT MELON |
| 7 | 3747 VERY LIGHT BLUE VIOLET |
| 210 | MEDIUM LAVENDER |
| ♥ | 3804 CYCLAMEN PINK |

STITCHING TUNES
"Chess," the London cast recording, which comes to you from the ABBA guys.

# Mom

## Possibilities

How cute would it be to stitch this on a onesie or bib for a new baby!
Or stitch it on your own jacket and change the letters to say "Me." Ha!
The alphabet on page 108 lets you replace "Mom" with any word. This
might be funky in all metallic threads, too.

## Truths

One of the reasons this design came about is my son Myles. It's so interesting
to me how having a child has changed my thought processes. To me this is
probably the most obvious tattoo . . . ever synonymous with sailors.

## Finishing

Pin and baste waste canvas to garment, being sure to skew it a bit so it's not
entirely straight. After stitching, wash the garment with the waste canvas
still attached, then pull out the waste threads one by one as described on
page 9 before drying the garment.

*mom [mom] noun*

*1. informal for mother 2. an honor*
*bestowed up on women who have a*
*great deal of patience and the ability*
*to juggle twenty things at once!*

### IMPORTANT STUFF

**Fabric**
Waste Canvas, 12 count: 6" (15 cm) wide
by 9" (23 cm) high.

**Thread**
DMC 6-strand Cotton Floss: 312 Very
Dark Baby Blue, 3708 Light Melon,
3756 Ultra Very Light Baby Blue.

**Stitch Density**
4 strands of thread over 2-by-2
group of canvas threads.

**Stitch Count**
77 wide by 42 high.

**Design Size**
6½" (16.5 cm) wide by 3½" (9 cm) high.

**Extras**
Denim jacket. *Note:* Use a sharp needle
for this project.

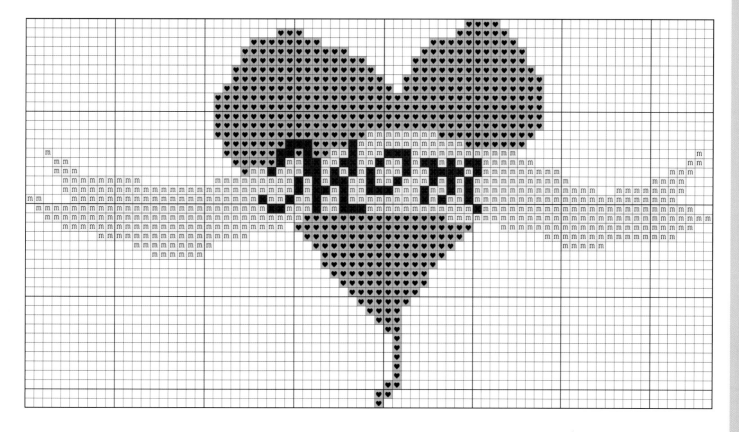

**DMC**

■ 3708 LIGHT MELON

■ 312 VERY DARK BABY BLUE

m 3756 ULTRA VERY LIGHT BABY BLUE

STITCHING TUNES
Patsy Cline's
Greatest Hits,
including "if
I could see the
world"—a classic.

# Spidey

## Possibilities

You need to check out Walker bags. Virtually any design could be stitched on one of these bright and versatile bags.

## Truths

To help see the holes in the mesh better, place something white under the bag.

## Finishing

Place design in upper right corner, 1" (2.5 cm) down from zipper and 1" (2.5 cm) from side of bag.

*Spidey [spi-dee] noun*

1. Peter Parker (aka Spiderman)

## IMPORTANT STUFF

### Fabric

Walker mesh bag (available at craft stores): about 32 count.

### Thread

DMC 6-strand Cotton Floss: 317 Pewter Gray, 762 Very Light Pearl Gray, 939 Very Dark Blue.

### Stitch Density

2 strands of thread over 2 mesh threads.

### Stitch Count

57 wide by 46 high.

### Design Size

3" (7.5 cm) wide by 3" (7.5 cm) high.

### Extras

9" x 12" (23 x 30.5 cm) Walker bag (available at art supply stores and online at www.walkerbag.com).

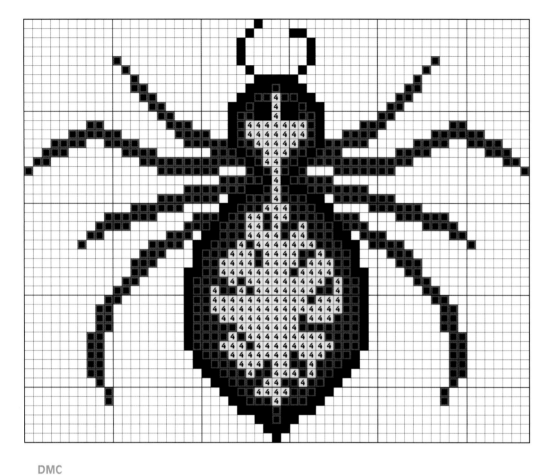

**DMC**

| 4 | 762 VERY LIGHT PEARL GRAY |
| --- | --- |
| ■ | 317 PEWTER GRAY |
| ■ | 939 VERY DARK BLUE |

STITCHING TUNES
Har Mar
Superstar,
"You Can
Feel ME."

# Compass

## Possibilities

What fun this design could be stitched up and put on the front of a travel journal; helping you record all of your journeys and adventures. And remember, as J.R.R. Tolkien said in his writings, "All who wander are not lost."

## Finishing

Press the design. To make the sandwich frame (see page 19), use the tin snips to cut the tube up the middle, flatten it out, and trim the wavy edges to 1" (2.5 cm) high. Cut two 9" (23 cm) lengths of this wavy edge. File all cut edges (wear work gloves to protect your hands). Clamp each metal piece on top of two of the wood strips and drill three holes equally spaced through all three layers. Place the top and bottom edges of the ironed design between a pair of wood strips, place the metal piece on top, and push a bolt through each hole (you may need to cut a small hole in the fabric to accommodate the bolt). Put a washer on each bolt, then a nut, and tighten securely.

compass [kuhm-puhs] noun

1. an instrument for determining directions

2. space within limits

**IMPORTANT STUFF**

**Fabric**

Wichelt Imports 28-count, 8" (20.5 cm) wide Lime Linen Stitch Band cut to 9" (23 cm) long.

**Thread**

DMC Handdyed 6-strand Cotton Floss: 498 Dark Red, 608 Bright Orange, 729 Medium Old Gold, 829 Very Dark Golden Olive, 939 Very Dark Navy Blue.

**Stitch Density**

2 strands of thread over 1 fabric thread.

**Stitch Count**

70 wide by 70 high.

**Design Size**

2½" (6.5 cm) wide and 2½" (6.5 cm) high.

**Extras**

4 strips of ¼" (6 mm) thick wood, each ⅝" x 8½" (1.5 x 21.5 cm); six ½" (1.3 cm) size 10 machine bolts with 6 washers and 6 nuts to fit; one 8" (20.5 cm) piece of galvanized steel duct pipe (available at hardware or improvement stores), preferably a connector T-pipe, which has a more wavy edge; tin snips; work gloves; steel file; ⅛" (3 mm) drill bit for metal and wood.

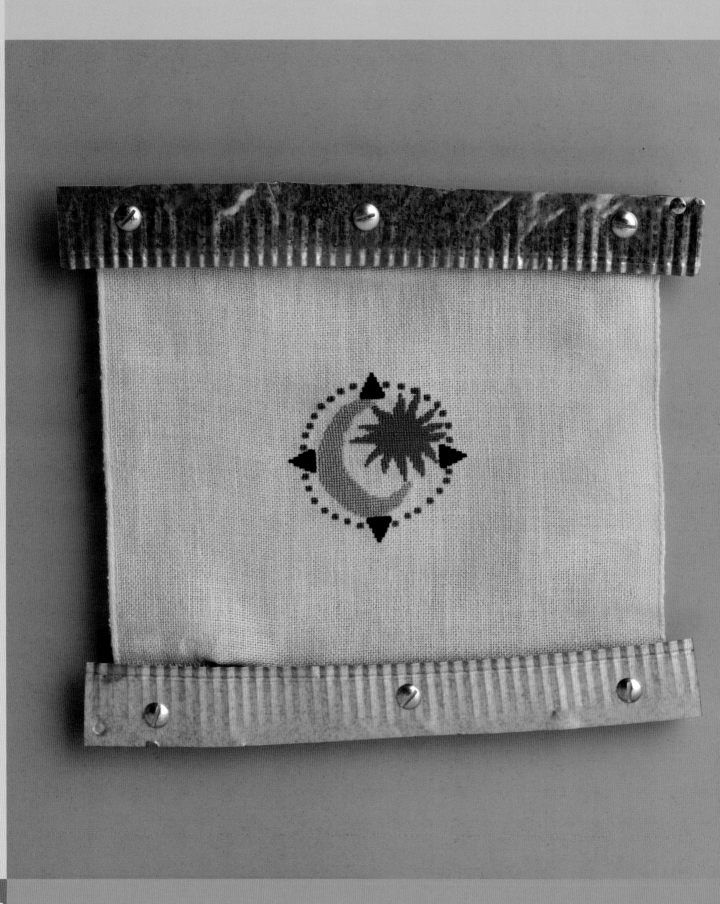

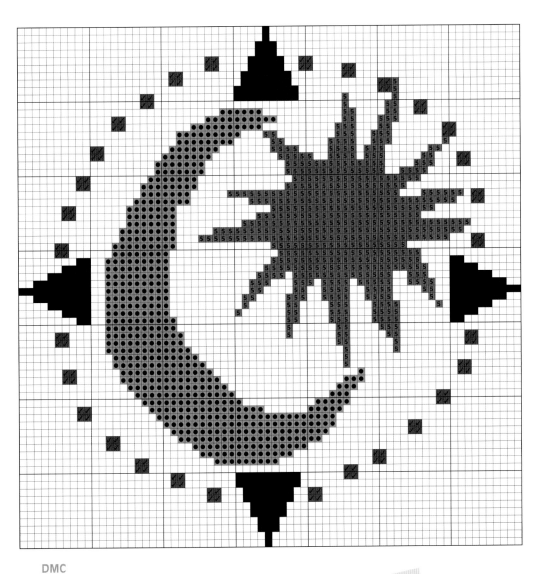

**DMC**

| | |
|---|---|
| **5** | 608 BRIGHT ORANGE |
| ● | 729 MEDIUM OLD GOLD |
| ■ | 939 VERY DARK NAVY BLUE |
| ✓ | 829 VERY DARK GOLDEN OLIVE |

STITCHING TUNES
Dion,
"The Wanderer."

# Yin Yang

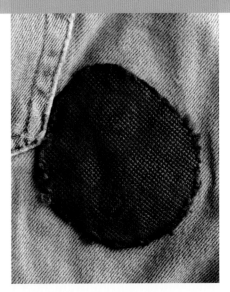

## Possibilities

For this design, I dyed the white Aida cloth in Procion MX cold-water dye that's colorfast (I can wash it whenever I want!). I have had several pieces of white Aida cloth in my stash since it's heyday in the 1980s. I have recently been dyeing lots of different fibers for fun, and threw this in a dye batch that had extra room. You can use any color fabric for this design; try 18 count for a smaller patch. You can do this in the "normal" black-and-white color scheme or choose your own fun colors: try lime and chocolate or purple and orange. Experiment!

## Finishing

Trim the Aida fabric ½" (1.3 cm) from the stitching. Machine or handstitch the patch to a pair of jeans, using a thread color that matches the Aida color. Trim the design fabric close to these last stitches. The Aida will fray and make the patch look even cooler!

### IMPORTANT STUFF

**Fabric**
14-count White Aida: 6" (15 cm) wide by 6" (15 cm) high.

**Thread**
DMC 6-strand Cotton Floss: 3607 Light Plum, 3801 Very Dark Melon.

**Stitch Density**
3 strands of thread over 1 fabric square.

**Stitch Count**
49 wide by 44 high.

**Design Size**
3¼" (8.5 cm) wide by 3" (7.5 cm) high.

**Extras**
Pair of old blue jeans.

*yin yang [yin yang] noun*
*1. a traditional symbol representing the Chinese theory of the forces of yin and yang  2. two principles, one negative, dark, and feminine (yin), and one positive, bright, and masculine (yang), whose interaction influences the destinies of creatures and things*

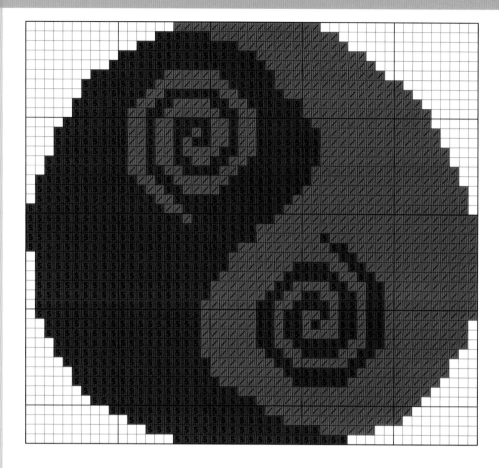

**DMC**

▨ 3801 VERY DARK MELON

▣ 3607 LIGHT PLUM

STITCHING TUNES

Sting,
"Ten Summoner's
Tales."

# Swirl

## Possibilities

I know that I have said this about a lot of projects, but this time I really mean it! You can use any color and type of thread for this—any! Have some fun and change the fabric color, too! Whoo hoo! The sky's the limit.

## Truths

Have you ever noticed a symbol that seems to be everywhere you go? The swirl is like that for me. I finally just gave into it, and I have intentionally put swirls everywhere. I figure there must be a reason for it; why fight it?

## Finishing

Stitch design on each fabric piece. Iron interfacing to back of each design fabric to prevent the shiny metal from showing through. Center each design over a button form and follow the manufacturer's instructions for finishing the buttons. Place a design button over the grommet at the base of the bag's strap, position a black button on the inside of the bag opposite the design button, and firmly sew the two together. Repeat for second button.

*swirl* [swurl] *noun*
*1. any curving, twisting line, shape, or form*
*2. confusion; disorder  3. the shape of something*
*rotating rapidly*

**IMPORTANT STUFF**

### Fabric
R&R Reproduction 30-count Hand-dyed Green Linen: 5" (12.5 cm) wide by 5" (12.5 cm) high. **Note:** Since you are making buttons, you will not need the extra 3" (7.5 cm) of fabric on all sides.

### Thread
The Thread Gatherer Silk'n'Colors: 189 Aurora's Flame.

### Stitch Density
2 strands of thread over 2 fabric threads.

### Stitch Count
27 wide by 29 high.

### Design Size
1¾" (4.5 cm) wide by 2" (5 cm) high.

### Extras
12" x 14" x 5" (30.5 x 35.5 x 12.5 cm) black mesh open tote Walker bag; 2 size 100 (2½"; 6.5 cm diameter) Half Ball Button Covers from Dritz; two 5" x 5" (12.5 x 12.5 cm) pieces of white light-weight iron-on interfacing; two ⅞" (2.2 cm) black buttons.

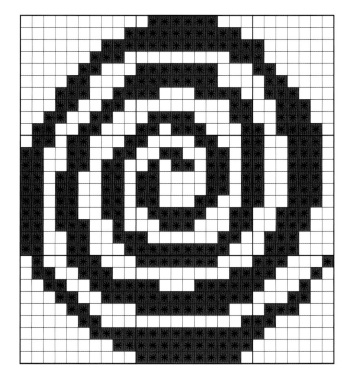

**Thread Gatherer Silk'n'Colors**
189 AURORA'S FLAME

STITCHING TUNES
Dianna Krall,
"Live in
Paris."

# Flutterby

## Possibilities

DMC has a line of variegated threads that give the look of a handdyed thread at a far less expensive price. These threads are washable so they could be used for any of the designs in this book or for any item that needs to be laundered.

## Finishing

Trim piece to 4¾" × 3½" (12 × 9 cm) with design centered. Pull out 5 linen threads around all sides to give a frayed look. Stitch onto mesh tote with 2 strands of 4050 floss, using long uneven stitches.

*flutterby [flu-ter-by]*

*1. not a word, but recognizable as a silly name for butterfly.*

## IMPORTANT STUFF

### Fabric
R&R Reproduction 32-count Handdyed Ink Spot Black Linen: 9" (23 cm) wide by 8" (20.5 cm) high.

### Thread
DMC 6-strand Cotton Floss: 211 Light Lavender, 3607 Light Plum, 3846 Light Bright Turquoise, 4050 variegated Roaming Pastures, 4080 variegated Daffodil Fields.

### Stitch Density
2 strands of thread over 2 fabric threads.

### Stitch Count
49 wide by 28 high.

### Design Size
3" (7.5 cm) wide by 1¾" (4.5 cm) high.

### Extras
11" x 9" (28 x 23 cm) Walker mesh tote (available at art supply stores or online at www.walkerbags.com).

**DMC**

| | |
|---|---|
| **2** | 4050 VARIEGATED ROAMING PASTURES |
| ♥ | 211 LIGHT LAVENDER |
| ⌐ | 4080 VARIEGATED DAFFODIL FIELDS |
| ✱ | 3607 LIGHT PLUM |
| m | 3846 LIGHT BRIGHT TURQUOISE |

STITCHING TUNES

Indigo Girls, "Rights of Passage."

# Windy

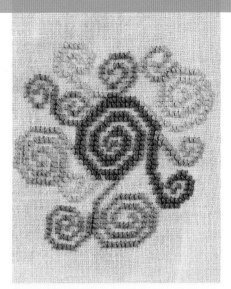

## Possibilities

There's something rewarding about stitching small designs like this one, especially when a stranger compliments your creation and wants to know where you purchased you hip top! If you are ever so inclined to stitch it again, try linen fabric or a pink or other color scheme.

## Finishing

After stitching is complete, wash the garment with the waste canvas still attached, then pull out the waste threads one by one as described on page 9 while the garment is still damp. Dry and iron garment.

*windy [win-dee] adjective*

*1. exposed to or swept by the wind*

*2. flatulent*

### IMPORTANT STUFF

**Fabric**
12-count waste canvas: 5" (12.5 cm) wide by 5" (12.5 cm) high.

**Thread**
DMC 6-strand Cotton Floss: 564 Very Light Jade, 597 Turquoise, 612 Light Drab Brown, 993 Very Light Aquamarine, 3812 Very Dark Sea Green.

**Stitch Density**
4 strands of thread over a 2-by-2 group of canvas threads.

**Stitch Count**
42 wide by 43 high.

**Design Size**
3½" (9 cm) wide by 3½" (9 cm) high.

**Extras**
Linen blouse.

**DMC**

W  612 LIGHT DRAB BROWN

B  993 VERY LIGHT AQUAMARINE

2  564 VERY LIGHT JADE

◣  597 TURQUOISE

●  3812 VERY DARK SEA GREEN

STITCHING TUNES
The Association,
"Greatest Hits."

# Lucky

## Possibilities
Wouldn't this make a wonderful gift for your best Irish pal?

## Finishing
Paint frame, then rub with sandpaper to create a vintage look. Press. Center and mount piece as described on page 18.

*lucky [luhk-ee] adjective*

*1. having or marked by good luck  2. occurring by chance; fortuitous  3. bringing or foretelling good luck, or supposed to do so: a lucky needle*

## IMPORTANT STUFF

### Fabric
R&R Reproduction 36-count Handdyed 18th-Century Brown Linen: 15" (38 cm) wide by 13" (33 cm) high.

### Thread
The Gentle Art Sampler Threads: 7040 Lexington Green, 0140 Blue Spruce, 7028 Grape Leaf, 1140 Oatmeal.

### Stitch Density
2 strands of thread over 2 fabric threads.

### Stitch Count
99 wide by 85 high.

### Design Size
5¾" (14.5 cm) wide by 4½" (11.5 cm) high.

### Extras
7½" x 9½" (19 x 24 cm) wood frame with a 4½" x 7" (11 x 18 cm) opening (available at craft stores); green acrylic or latex paint; fine sandpaper.

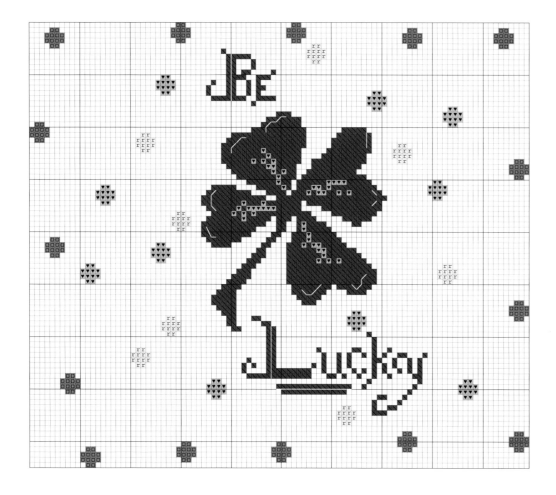

| | Sampler Threads | DMC alternate |
|---|---|---|
| ☐ | 7028 GRAPE LEAF | 469 AVOCADO GREEN |
| ◩ | 0140 BLUE SPRUCE | 3346 HUNTER GREEN |
| ♥ | 7040 LEXINGTON GREEN | 470 LIGHT AVOCADO GREEN |
| r | 1140 OATMEAL | 746 OFF WHITE |

NOTE: WORK ALL BACKSTITCHES WITH OATMEAL.

STITCHING TUNES
The Chieftains,
"Water From
the Well."

# Surfer Girl

## Possibilities

This bag is sized like a gift bag, but the design would be great on a beach-size bag. Or use waste canvas and stitch it to a big denim bag made out of an old pair of Levi's! Every time you see the bag, it will remind you that it's time to go to the beach again. Remember all the great times you've had there.

## Finishing

There's nothing more to do!

*surfer [surf-r] noun*

*1. someone who engages in surfboarding*

*2. one who casually looks at something offering numerous options, especially the Internet or television*

## IMPORTANT STUFF

### Fabric
Jute bag with about 14 count: 5" (12.5 cm) wide by 9½" (24 cm) high. **Note:** The fabric used for this bag is not evenweave.

### Thread
DMC 6-strand Cotton Floss: 550 Very Dark Violet, 3840 Light Lavender Blue, 3862 Dark Mocha Beige.

### Stitch Density
4 strands of thread over 1 fabric thread.

### Stitch Count
61 wide by 60 high.

### Design Size
3¾" (9.5 cm) wide by 4¼" (11 cm) high.

### Extras
5" x 9½" (12.5 x 24 cm) jute bag.

**DMC**

- ■ 550 VERY DARK VIOLET
- ● 3840 LIGHT LAVENDER BLUE
- 5 3862 DARK MOCHA BEIGE

STITCHING TUNES

The Beach Boys, "Surfin' Safari."

stuff [stuhf] ~ noun

1. material to be worked upon or to be used in making something  2. property, as personal belongings or equipment; things  3. Worthless objects

# stuff

## These designs, like most in this book,

are meant to adorn the stuff around you. They'll give you an idea of where your stitching can go and the different surfaces you can stitch on. They'll also show you some creative ways to finish your needlework. Put that collection of beads, tissue paper, watch gears, broken dishes, or whatever you have stashed away for later use, to work!

# Bloomer

## Possibilities

The screen I used is about 15 count, but you should know that screen counts can vary. Since the hardware industry has no demand for this information, you need to count the number of "threads" there are in an inch (take a ruler with you). The measurements given here are based on my model—if you're unsure about the size, begin with a larger piece of screen (it will get trimmed anyway).

Not interested in stitching on screen? This would be beautiful on a piece of bright yellow (or white) linen fabric and traditionally framed.

## Truths

The first time it occurred to me that screen might be an interesting thing to stitch upon was when my husband and I were up to our eyeballs in a never-ending home restoration project. We had purchased a very run down 1883 Queen Anne house in historic Riverside, California. It was a cool location, but our house was definitely a sore spot on the block. It was going to cost a small fortune to install modern screens on the windows, so we made them the old-fashioned way. My handy husband built frames, and we rolled in the screen with the spline. As we worked, it popped into my head that stitching on the screen could be a fun way to repair the little pulls and tears our cats managed to put in the screens—I sure didn't want to replace them again! So, I cut off a chunk of screen, grabbed several types of fibers, and started experimenting. Since then I have stitched a lot on screen and the results are always very nice! It's also great for teaching kids—just set them up with a needle and thread, get them started, and let them go to town. It's wonderful to see what they create, and it often gives them the desire to do more!

*bloomer [bloo-mer] noun*

*1. a plant that blooms   2. a person who attains full maturity and competence   3. loose trousers gathered at the knee*

**IMPORTANT STUFF**

**Fabric**

About 30-count nylon screen (available at hardware stores): 8" (20.5 cm) wide by 8" (20.5 cm) high.

**Thread**

Caron Collection 3-strand Handdyed Watercolours: 237 Apple Blossom, 084 African Sunset, 085 Antique Brass, 211 Cucumber, 236 Appalachia.

DMC 6-strand Cotton Floss: 604 Light Cranberry.

**Stitch Density**

1 strand of thread over 1 screen "thread."

**Stitch Count**

67 wide by 68 high.

**Design Size**

About 4½" (11 cm) wide by 4" (10 cm) high tall.

**Extras**

34 Swarovski 6mm round fuchsia crystals; 2 strips of wood, each 7" x 1" (18 x 2.5 cm); two 1" (2.5 cm) bolts; 2 washers (the ones shown are pieces from a molder/shaping machine in my husband's workshop; you can use regular washers or any found object with a hole in the center); 2 nuts to fit (available at hardware stores).

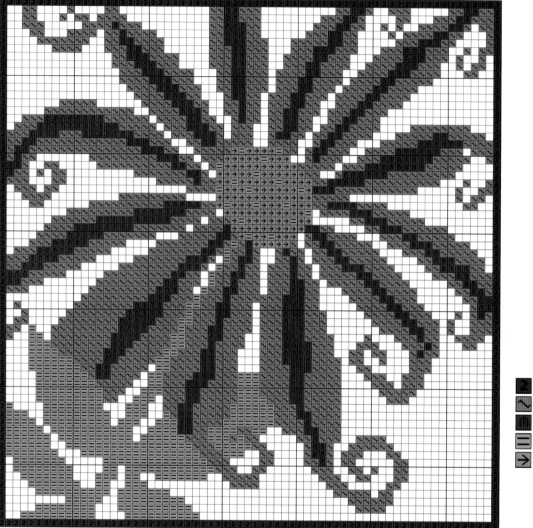

**Watercolours**

| | |
|---|---|
| 236 | APPALACHIA |
| 237 | APPLE BLOSSOM |
| 084 | AFRICAN SUNSET |
| 211 | CUCUMBER |
| 085 | ANTIQUE BRASS |

## Finishing

When the stitching is complete, sew on the crystals with 2 strands of DMC #604 in a loose whipstitch, making an effort to keep the beads relatively even. Start at one lower corner, attach a bead, run the needle 3 squares away, then attach another bead. Continue this pattern to the opposite corner to create a sparkly border for your early bloomer! Make a sandwch frame with the wood and hardware as described on page 19.

STITCHING TUNES
The movie soundtrack to "singin' in the rain"...a classic.

# No Fly

## Truths

The idea for this design came from the fly swatter itself. I love stitching on screen and have done several designs on fly swatters that relate to flies or the word "fly." Brainstorming sessions go like this: I say to my sister or husband, "I really want to do another design on a fly swatter, do you have any ideas?" Invariably they do, they're fountains of ideas actually (it takes a village, you know). "No fly zone" came from my sister Sarah; everything else is all me (ha!). This fly swatter has an antique look and is made by a company in France, called Combrican. I first saw this type of swatter in a specialty hardware store but have seen variations of it online as well. But any swatter with wire or nylon screen will do. Now you can swat your flies in style!

## Finishing

Center and stitch the design. The frame is finished before you even begin stitching! What fun!

*No-Fly Zone [noh-flahy zohn] noun*
*1. an area over which no military flights are allowed*
*[Origin: 1991]*

### IMPORTANT STUFF

**Fabric**
Wire screen of a fly swatter.

**Thread**
DMC Size 5 pearl cotton: 939 Very Dark Navy Blue, 946 Medium Burnt Orange.
***Note:*** Use shorter length threads to avoid fraying and bury all of your starting and ending thread tails.

**Stitch Density**
1 strand of thread over 1 screen "thread."

**Stitch Count**
51 wide by 56 high.

**Design Size**
Depends on the count of the fly-swatter screen.

**Extras**
1 fly swatter.

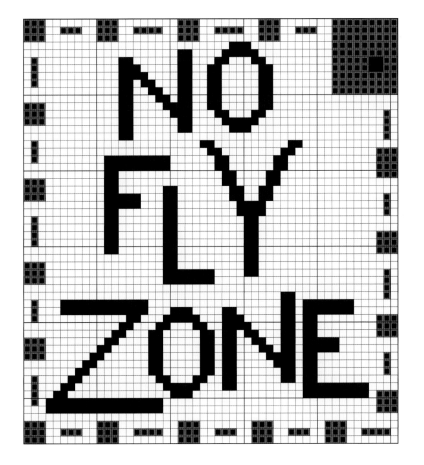

**DMC size 5 pearl cotton**

■ 946 MEDIUM BURNT ORANGE

■ 939 VERY DARK NAVY BLUE

STITCHING TUNES
Frank Sinatra,
"The Very Good
Years" with a
recording of "Fly
Me to the Moon."

# Home

## Truths

I grew up in a family from the Midwest that very rarely traveled so far that they couldn't make it home the same day to sleep in their own beds. When a friend of mine told me this quote, I simply had to come up with a design for it.

## Finishing

Fold the fabric edges under ½" (1.3 cm) from the sides of the design and 1" (2.5 cm) from the top and bottom, forming a square. Press. Tack design fabric to pillow with buttons (use the buttons provided or buttons rescued from an old blouse or other funky vintage buttons).

*home [bohm] noun*

*1. the place in which one's domestic affections are centered  2. a person's native place or own country  3. the base at which the batter stands and which a base runner must reach safely in order to score a run*

### IMPORTANT STUFF

**Fabric**

Wichelt Imports 28-count Handdyed Summer Sky Jobelan: 11" (28 cm) wide by 11" (28 cm) high.

**Thread**

Weeks Dye Works 6-strand Cotton Floss: Whitewash, Buttercup, Bordeaux, Cocoa, Blue Topaz, Bark, Mimosa, Bayberry.

**Stitch Density**

2 strands of thread over 2 fabric threads.

**Stitch Count**

69 wide by 67 high.

**Design Size**

5" (12.5 cm) wide by 4¾" (12 cm) high.

**Extras**

9½" x 9½" (24 x 24 cm) pillow (pillow shown is a Wall Wearable Pillow from Trail Creek Farm).

| Weeks Dye Works | | DMC alternate | |
|---|---|---|---|
| ✳ | BLUE TOPAZ | 3810 | DARK TURQUOISE |
| m | MIMOSA | 722 | LIGHT ORANGE SPICE |
| ⌐ | WHITEWASH | 1109 | ECRU |
| ■ | BORDEAUX | 814 | DARK GARNET RED |
| ╱ | BUTTERCUP | 3047 | LIGHT YELLOW BEIGE |
| ▨ | COCOA | 610 | VERY DARK DRAB BROWN |
| ▦ | BARK | 935 | DARK AVOCADO GREEN |
| | (also backstitches for window panes) | | |
| ★ | BAYBERRY | 991 | DARK AQUAMARINE |
| | (also backstitches for flower stems) | | |

STITCHING TUNES
The Dixie Chicks,
"Fly" or "Home;"
some of the best
"chick" music
around!

# Hip Hip!

## Truths

Hip hip. I grew up in southern Illinois and went to high school in Centralia. We were the Centralia Orphans. Yes, that's right, our mascot was an Orphan. No other school in the U.S.A. can toot this horn! And, to make this an even better story as a girl athlete, I was an ORPHAN ANNIE. No kidding, frilly tennis bloomers and all. So, who wouldn't have a lasting love for their school and shout hip, hip, hooray when the home team does well? It's one of my favorite facts from my past—always a conversation starter!

## Finishing

With Cilantro, work random straight stitches in the center of the second "o" in hooray. Cut 2 triangular pieces of wool, each 17" (43 cm) long and 7" (18 cm) at the highest part. Fold under ⅛" (3 mm) from the stitching on all sides and press. If necessary, trim the corners on the wrong side so that they don't show on the front. Tack each design corner to one of the wool triangles, using the four tiny buttons and African Sunset thread. Sew the two triangles of wool together using Cilantro thread and a blanket stitch (see page 109). Sew the assorted raspberry buttons randomly along the short side of the triangular piece. Voilà, a funky banner for your room!

*hooray [huh-rey]*
*interjection*

*1. variant of hurrah  2. used as an*
*exclamation of pleasure, approval,*
*elation, or victory*

### IMPORTANT STUFF

**Fabric**
R&R Reproduction 20-count Handdyed Sibling Summer Sky Linen: 12" (30.5 cm) wide by 10" (25.5 cm) high.

**Thread**
Caron Collection Wildflowers: 208 Tangerine; 190 Fraises duBois; 215 Cilantro; 084 African Sunset.

**Stitch Density**
1 strand of thread over 1 fabric thread.

**Stitch Count**
116 wide by 69 high.

**Design Size**
5¾" (14.5 cm) wide by 3½" (9 cm) high.

**Extras**
1 fat quarter (about 20" by 20" [51 by 51 cm]) handdyed wool (#3338 Pumpkin from Weeks Dye Works); handdyed buttons from Hillcreek Designs (#3009D Shades of Raspberry (18 assorted colors and sizes) and #3019-TW Shades of Orange (4 of the brightest and smallest).

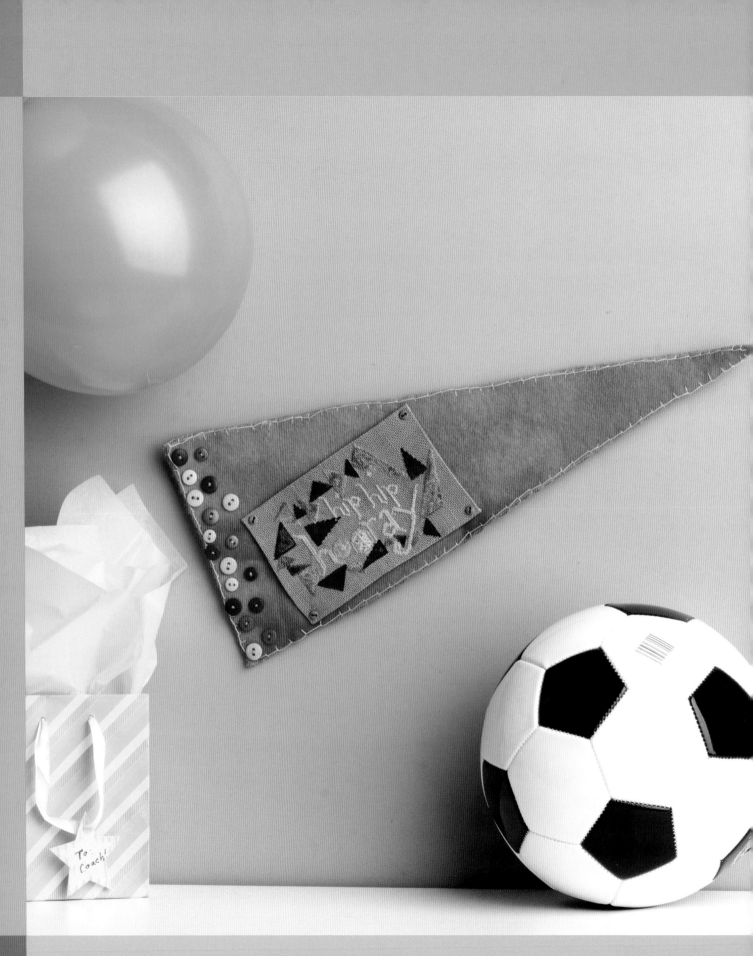

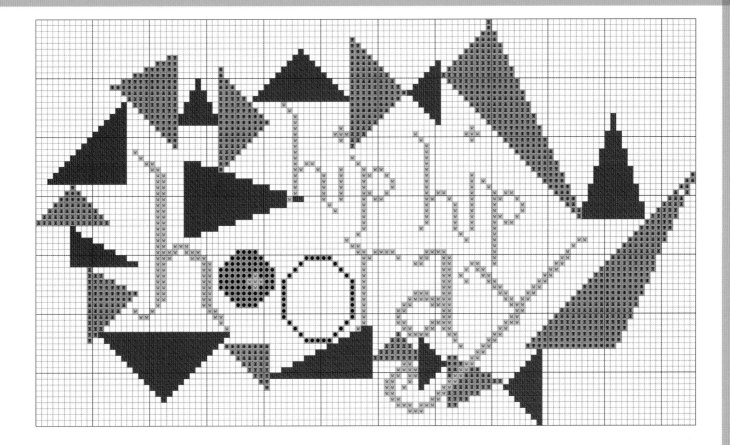

| | Caron Wildflowers | DMC alternate | |
|---|---|---|---|
| W | 215 CILANTRO | 3819 | LIGHT MOSS GREEN |
| | 084 AFRICAN SUNSET | 3804 | DARK CYCLAMEN PINK |
| ∓ | 190 FRAISES DUBOIS | 604 | LIGHT CRANBERRY |
| ● | 208 TANGERINE | 741 | MEDIUM TANGERINE |

STITCHING TUNES
Elvis Costello,
"King of
America."

# Three Bracelets

Here are three easy bracelets to stitch on nylon screen. The design size will depend on the exact count of your screen. Adjust the length if necessary to fit your wrist.

## POLKA

### Truth

I have always been a collector of cool clothes, wonderful beads, and original jewelry, so it's inevitable that I'd combine them with embroidery. Sew the same buttons onto a favorite bag or sweater for a fun fashion combo!

## Finishing

Trim screen to one thread beyond outermost stitching on all sides. Attach the larger jump ring to the center of one short end and the smaller jump ring to the opposite end. Using the wire, make a fastener in the shape of a U with the ends curled inward and 1" (2.5 cm) long. Leave one end of the fastener somewhat open until it is attached to the small jump ring.

*[pohl-kuh] noun*

*1. a Bohemian dance with three steps and a hop in fast time  2. a piece of music for such a dance or in its rhythm.*

**IMPORTANT STUFF**

**Fabric**
Nylon screen of about 18 count: 5" (12.5 cm) wide by 9" (23 cm) high for each bracelet.

**Thread**
Caron Collection 3-strand Watercolours: 160 Night Sky, 188 Lime Rickey.

**Stitch Density**
1 strand of thread over 1 screen "thread."

**Stitch Count**
118 wide by 20 high.

**Design Size**
About 1½" (3.8 cm) wide by 6½" (16.5 cm) high.

**Extras**
Five ⅝" (1.5 cm) wide sterling enamel buttons (buttons shown are Lime Circle Spots from Gita Maria); 6" (15 cm) of 14-gauge half-hard sterling silver wire; one 10 mm jump ring; one 6 mm jump ring.

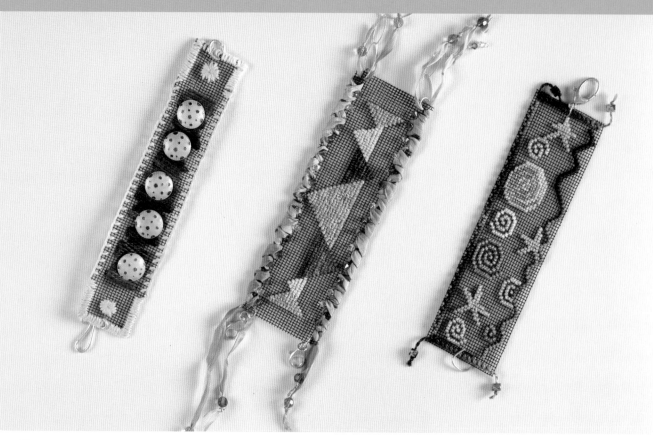

## Polka

### Caron Watercolours
— 160 NIGHT SKY (straight stitches)
— 188 LIME RICKEY (straight stitches)
**3** GITA MARIA BUTTONS

STITCHING TUNES
Squirrel Nut
Zippers,
"Perennial
Favorites."

# UNIVERSE

## Possibilities

I debated over where to stitch this design. I originally designed it to be stitched onto the hem of a favorite pair of jeans, but it became a bracelet when I needed a gift for a certain galaxy gal friend. I like it as a bracelet, but I still think it would be great on a pair of jeans. If you continued the pattern, it could become a border for a celestial quote: "Twinkle, twinkle, little star . . . ," or the Betty Davis line, "Don't let's ask for the moon, we've got the stars," or an Emerson quote, "When it is darkest, men see the stars," or maybe Casey Casem's sign-off from his weekly billboard countdown, "Keep your feet on the ground, but keep reaching for the stars."

## Finishing

Be sure to hide all the thread tails by burying them into the backs of previously worked stitches and trimming them closely, except for the tails at the start and end of each cross-stitch over 2 rows. Trim the screen very close to the stitching but don't cut through the nylon squares that have stitches. Don't leave sharp mesh edges; this is tricky and requires a bit of time, sharp scissors, and a bright light. Attach the lobster claw to the 6mm jump ring, then attach the ring to the screen, centered and 3 squares from the edge. Center the 10mm jump ring on the opposite end of the screen to complete the clasp. Tie a small knot close to the surface of the design for each of the remaining thread tails; thread 1 square bead onto each tail and tie another small knot ⅝" (1.5 cm) from first knot. Trim tails ¼" (6 mm) from last knot.

*universe [yoo-nuh-vurs] noun*
*1. the totality of known or supposed objects and*
*phenomena throughout space 2. a world or sphere in*
*which something exists or prevails: "this is the greatest*
*design in the whole universe" 3. everything that exists*
*anywhere—earth, planets, sun, stars, etc.*

**IMPORTANT STUFF**

**Fabric**
Nylon screen of about 18 count: 5" (12.5 cm) wide by 9" (23 cm) high for each bracelet.

**Thread**
Caron Collection 3-strand Handdyed Watercolours: 204 Umbria, 229 Oasis, 241 Shenandoah, 243 Pesto.

**Stitch Density**
1 strand of thread over 1 screen "thread."

**Stitch Count**
28 wide by 89 high.

**Design Size**
About 1½" (3.8 cm) wide by 6" (15 cm) high.

**Extras**
1 silver-plated 28mm long, round lobster claw finding; one 10mm jump ring; one 6 mm jump ring. **Note:** Nearly any closure toggles or lobster-claw clasps will work.

## Universe

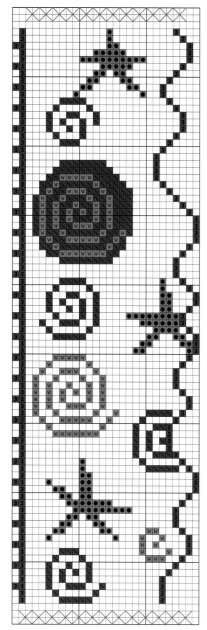

### Caron Watercolours

| | |
|---|---|
| ◼ | 241 SHENANDOAH |
| ● | 243 PESTO |
| W | 229 OASIS |
| 3 | 204 UMBRIA |
| ▭ | 204 UMBRIA OVER 2 MESH THREADS |

(leave 4" tail at start and end of each row)

## Pyramids

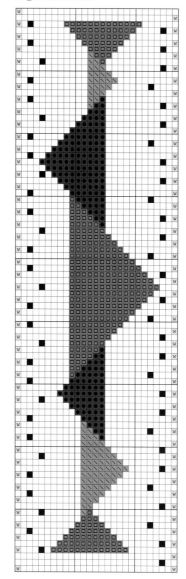

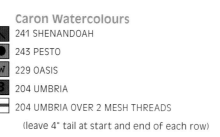

### Caron Watercolours

| | |
|---|---|
| ◼ | BICONE CRYSTALS IN |
| | INDOCOLITE, LIGHT AZORE, AND INDIAN SAPPHIRE |
| ▫ | 234 CELESTIAL BLUE |
| ● | 235 TANZANITE |
| ◹ | 181 OCEAN BLUE |

### The Thread Gatherer Silk'n'Ribbon

| | |
|---|---|
| W | SR048 PEARLED BLUES |

# PYRAMIDS

## Truths

Stitching on screen is relatively simple—and the only tricky part is hiding your thread tails on the back so that they don't show through to the front. Also, the screen will make threads fray more easily, so use shorter-length threads than you'd normally use.

## Possibilities

What a fun gift this will be for your friend who has everything! I guarantee she doesn't have a piece of jewelry like this! Colors are easily interchangeable in case you or your friend is a green fanatic or always wears black and red. Every time I wear my bracelet I get many compliments and always get asked where I found it. People are surprised to learn that I made it, that it is cross-stitched, and that it was stitched on screen! Delightful!

## Finishing

Trim the screen to 2" × 6" (5 × 15 cm). Whipstitch the ribbon along each long edge, beginning at one corner and working into every fifth hole, leaving a 3" (7.5 cm) tail at each end. Repeat the stitching, going in the opposite direction and stitching between the previous stitches. Thread two 6mm round Swarovski crystals on each ribbon tail so that each corner has 1 Indo-colite and 1 Light Sapphire bead per ribbon tail; tie a small knot at the end of each ribbon and decoratively trim (the tails do not need to be the same length). Using a jump ring, attach a 5 mm length of chain to each corner of one short end of screen, placed about 3 squares in from the corner. At the opposite short end, attach a lobster claw to each corner with a jump ring in the same manner. To wear, fasten the lobster claws to the chains.

### pyramid [pir-uh-mid] noun

*1. in ancient Egypt a quadrilateral masonry mass having smooth, steeply sloping sides meeting at an apex, used as a tomb 2. a solid having a polygonal base, and triangular sides that meet in a point*

## IMPORTANT STUFF

### Fabric
Nylon screen of about 18 count: 5" (12.5 cm) wide by 9" (23 cm) high for each bracelet.

### Thread
Caron Collection 3-strand Handdyed Watercolours: 234 Celestial Blue, 235 Tanzanite, 181 Ocean Blue.
The Thread Gatherer Silk'n'Ribbon: 7mm SR 048 Pearled Blues.

### Stitch Density
1 strand of thread over 1 screen "thread."

### Stitch Count
27 wide by 90 high.

### Design Size
About 1½" (3.8 cm) wide by 5" (12.5 cm) high.

### Extras
12 each of 4mm Bicone Swarovski Crystals in Indocolite, Light Azore, and Indian Sapphire; 4 each of 6mm round Indocolite and light sapphire crystals; two 17 x 6 mm silver-plated lobster claw findings; 10 cm length of silver-plated medium to large link jewelry chain; four 7mm jump rings.

## Blanket Stitch

Bring the threaded needle out of the background and move it the desired number of threads to the right (1 thread shown here). Insert the needle into the background the desired number of threads above (1 thread shown here) and back out 1 thread below where it originally came out, being careful to keep the needle on top of the working thread. Working to the right, continue to insert the needle in and out of the background in this manner at regular intervals.

## Eyelet Stitch

Bring the threaded needle out of the background at the center of where you want the eyelet to begin, then back into the background to the upper left the desired number of threads (2 threads shown here). Insert the needle in the next thread to the right, then out again at the center of the eyelet. Continue working in a circular manner until every background thread has been worked, ending up where you began.

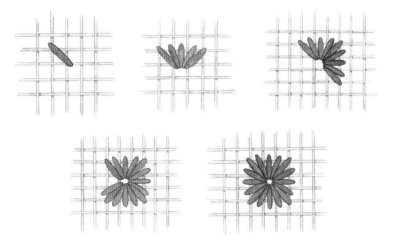

## Straight Stitch

Bring the threaded needle in and out of the background as desired to create stitches of the desired length. Straight stitches can be vertical, horizontal, or diagonal.

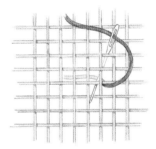

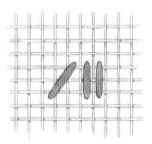

## Whipstitch

Working along the edge of the fabric background, bring the threaded needle behind the background, then up the desired number of stitches from the edge (2 threads shown here). Move the desired number of stitches to the right (or left), repeat this motion at regular intervals.

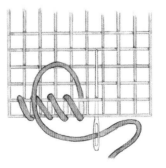

# sources

**The Caron Collection**
55 Old South Ave.
Stratford, CT 06615
www.caronc-net.com

**Combrichon S.A.** (fly swatters)
114 allée de Forquevaux
B.P. 126
01601 Trevoux Cedex
France
www.combrichon.com

**Crescent Colours**
4100 South Fremont Ave., Ste. 110
Tucson, AZ 85714
www.crescentcolours.com

**The DMC Corporation**
77 South Hackensack Ave., Bldg. 10F
South Kearny, NJ 07032
www.dmc.com

**The Gentle Art**
PO Box 670
New Albany, OH 43054
www.thegentleart.com

**Gita Maria**
PO Box 918
Gold Beach, OR 97444
www.GitaMaria.com

**Hillcreek Designs** (buttons)
10159 Buena Vista Ave.
Santee, CA 92071
www.hillcreekdesigns.com

**Hog River Frames**
Available from Eastside Mouldings
401 S. 7th St., Unit 5
Akron, PA 17501
www.eastsidemouldings.com

**Kreinik Manufacturing Company Inc.**
1708 Gihon Rd.
Parkersburg, WV 26102
www.kreinik.com

**R & R Reproductions**
wedyeforyou@aol.com

**National Supply** (beads and beading supplies)
9666 Olive Blvd., Ste. 145
St. Louis, MO 63132
www.nationalsupply.com

**Nichole Crafts** (jute bags)
www.nicholecrafts.com

**Trail Creek Farm**
1355 15th Rd.
Lyons, KS 67554
www.trailcreekfarm.com

**Walker Bags**
81 Dorman Ave.
San Francisco, CA 94124
www.walkerbags.com

**Wichelt Imports Inc.**
N162 Hwy. 35
Stoddard, WI 54658
www.wicheltimports.com

# Create Beautiful Designs

## WITH THESE INSPIRING RESOURCES FROM INTERWEAVE PRESS

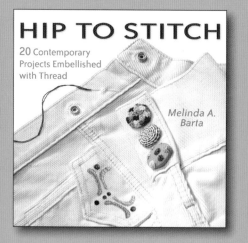
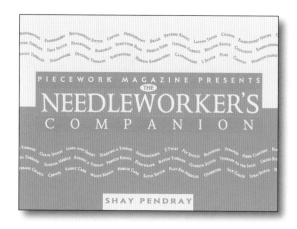
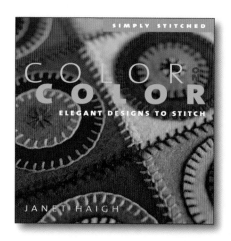
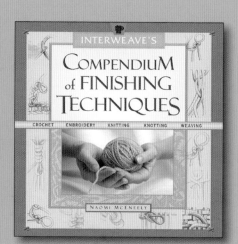